W9-CHO-837

3 4047 11612 0028

813.6
KHA

Bloom's Guides:

KHaled Hosseini's
The Kite Runner

DISCARDED

Bloom's

GUIDES

Khaled Hosseini's

The Kite Runner

CURRENTLY AVAILABLE

The Adventures of Huckleberry Finn
All the Pretty Horses
Animal Farm
The Autobiography of Malcolm X
The Awakening
The Bell Jar
Beloved
Beowulf
Brave New World
The Canterbury Tales
Catch-22
The Catcher in the Rye
The Chosen
The Crucible
Cry, the Beloved Country
Death of a Salesman
Fahrenheit 451
Frankenstein
The Glass Menagerie
The Grapes of Wrath
Great Expectations
The Great Gatsby
Hamlet
The Handmaid's Tale
Heart of Darkness
The House on Mango Street
I Know Why the Caged Bird Sings
The Iliad
Invisible Man
Jane Eyre

The Kite Runner
Lord of the Flies
Macbeth
Maggie: A Girl of the Streets
The Member of the Wedding
The Metamorphosis
Native Son
Night
1984
The Odyssey
Oedipus Rex
Of Mice and Men
One Hundred Years of Solitude
Pride and Prejudice
Ragtime
A Raisin in the Sun
The Red Badge of Courage
Romeo and Juliet
The Scarlet Letter
A Separate Peace
Slaughterhouse-Five
Snow Falling on Cedars
The Stranger
A Streetcar Named Desire
The Sun Also Rises
A Tale of Two Cities
The Things They Carried
To Kill a Mockingbird
Uncle Tom's Cabin
The Waste Land
Wuthering Heights

DERBY PUBLIC LIBRARY
313 Elizabeth St.
Derby, CT 06418

Bloom's

GUIDES

Khaled Hosseini's
The Kite Runner

Edited & with an Introduction
by Harold Bloom

BLOOM'S
LITERARY CRITICISM
An imprint of Infobase Publishing

Bloom's Guides: The Kite Runner

Copyright © 2009 by Infobase Publishing

Introduction © 2009 by Harold Bloom

All rights reserved. No part of this book may be reproduced or utilized in any form or by any means, electronic or mechanical, including photocopying, recording, or by any information storage or retrieval systems, without permission in writing from the publisher. For information contact:

Bloom's Literary Criticism
An imprint of Infobase Publishing
132 West 31st Street
New York, NY 10001

Library of Congress Cataloging-in-Publication Data
The kite runner / edited and with an introduction by Harold Bloom.
    p. cm. — (Bloom's guides)
  Includes bibliographical references and index.
  ISBN 978-1-60413-199-4 (acid-free paper) 1. Hosseini, Khaled. Kite runner. 2. Afghanistan—In literature. I. Title. II. Series.

PS3608.O832K5835 2009
813'.6—dc22

                                        2008035050

Bloom's Literary Criticism books are available at special discounts when purchased in bulk quantities for businesses, associations, institutions, or sales promotions. Please call our Special Sales Department in New York at (212) 967-8800 or (800) 322-8755.

You can find Bloom's Literary Criticism on the World Wide Web at
http://www.chelseahouse.com

Contributing Editor: Pamela Loos
Cover design by Takeshi Takahashi
Printed in the United States of America
Bang EJB 10 9 8 7 6 5 4 3 2 1
This book is printed on acid-free paper.

All links and Web addresses were checked and verified to be correct at the time of publication. Because of the dynamic nature of the Web, some addresses and links may have changed since publication and may no longer be valid.

DERBY PUBLIC LIBRARY
313 Elizabeth St.
Derby, CT 06418Contents

DERBY PUBLIC LIBRARY
313 Elizabeth St.
Derby, CT 06418

HAROLD BLOOM

My idol, Dr. Samuel Johnson, greatest of all literary critics, urged us to clear our minds of cant. "Cant" in this sense means stock catchwords in temporary fashion, ephemeral pieties, affected attitudes, however ostensibly humane. Oscar Wilde, who had nothing in common with Johnson, but is another of my intellectual guides, told us that "all bad poetry is sincere," and so are most novels and plays that will not last.

I pursue my now quarter-century-old project of Bloom's Literary Criticism knowing well that for the enterprise to survive, it must compromise with the marketplace. Johnson's *Lives of the English Poets* is my precursor. The booksellers (then publishers as well as vendors) enumerated the poets, and Johnson was free to speak his mind and tell his truth. I assert the same freedom. *The Kite Runner* is in fashion and serves the needs of our moment. We have been fighting in Afghanistan for seven years now, and the recent resurgence of the Taliban means we may be embattled there beyond the horizon of my likely span of life (I am seventy-eight as I write). Someday we will be out of Afghanistan and no one will return to reading *The Kite Runner*, which is a grindingly sincere narrative in the shape of a memoir.

All of *The Kite Runner*, like all of, say, Isabel Allende or J.K. Rowling is composed in clichés. I open the book at random and confront smiles that "wilt," lines "etched" into aging faces, "things . . . cooling off again" between former friends, "gnawing" of nails, all on pages 92–93. Though I have just compelled myself to read through the book, I cannot regard it as *writing*. That there is redeeming social value is unquestionable. Many people have gotten through it who cannot absorb serious scholarship about Afghanistan or even responsible reportage. But my own function cannot be to commend mere sincerity or public utility. Literary fiction requires mastery of language and its nuances, sustained cognition, skill in characterization.

What can be used necessarily can be used up. One does not expect every attempt at a novel to give us Joseph Conrad's *Nostromo* or *The Portrait of a Lady* by Henry James. But characters cannot be only names upon a page, and the interests of art cannot be set aside without irreparable loss to the cry and image of the human.

DERBY PUBLIC LIBRARY
313 Elizabeth St.
Derby, CT 06418

 Biographical Sketch

Khaled Hosseini has shown an increasing number of readers what it means to be from Afghanistan. In a post-9/11 world, interest in the nation remains high. To some, Afghanistan seems a harsh, barren land deeply affected by violence. Hosseini's *The Kite Runner*, however, gives a vision of what Afghanistan was before its association as a haven for terrorists. The book lends a human face to the country's citizens, witnesses to the many changes that have gripped their homeland.

Hosseini was born in Kabul, Afghanistan, on March 4, 1965, during what is sometimes referred to as the country's golden years (the 1960s and 1970s). By 1970, Hosseini, the oldest of five children, moved with his family to Iran, when his diplomat father was assigned by the Afghan foreign ministry to work in the nation's embassy in Tehran. The family lived there for three years and then returned to Kabul, where they had a comfortable life and an array of intellectual and artist friends. Hosseini's mother taught history and Farsi (or Persian) at a girls' school, and Hosseini read much Persian poetry, as well as translations of American and other Western novels, and heard many Afghan stories from his family and the radio; in grade school he began writing short stories.

In 1973, the nation entered a period of instability, when the monarch was overthrown, and it was not completely clear what might follow. Three years later, Hosseini's father was assigned to the Afghan embassy in Paris, so the family moved again. Further unrest rocked Afghanistan in 1978 in the form of a Marxist coup and the overthrow of the president. In a time marked by violence and killing, Hosseini's father feared that his family members' lives were at risk. The situation worsened in 1979 when the Soviet Union launched its invasion of Afghanistan. The Hosseinis were granted political asylum in the United States and moved to San Jose, California, in 1980. Hosseini learned English relatively quickly, but the move to the United States required the family to make great adjustments.

Hosseini's parents lost their careers; initially the family was on welfare, and then his parents took low-level jobs.

By 1984, Hosseini had graduated Independence High School in San Jose and then enrolled in Santa Clara University. While he had previously wanted to become a writer, he instead entered the medical profession, knowing he was good at science and deciding that he wanted to work with people and do something that mattered. In 1989, he started medical school at the University of California at San Diego and graduated four years later. He worked as an internist and in the internal medicine department at the Permanente Medical Group in Mountain View, California. Not quite ready to give up on writing, Hosseini started producing short stories again, and when he heard that the Taliban (the fundamentalist group that controlled much of Afghanistan from 1996 through 2001) had banned kite flying in his native land, he wrote a story about two boys who enjoyed that pastime together.

That story was later expanded into a novel and completed in midsummer 2002; by September, Hosseini had a publisher. Just prior to the book's release, he returned to visit Afghanistan, his first trip there in twenty-seven years. In 2007, he wrote in the *Guardian* that in some ways he saw that trip as "a marriage of the horrific and the poetic." Buildings had been reduced to rubble, trees cut down, and he was mobbed by children begging. The Taliban was gone, but a majority of people were living in abject poverty.

The Kite Runner received a positive initial response yet gained more attention when it later came out in paperback and was enthusiastically received by many book-club readers. It became an international bestseller and has been published in 42 languages. In 2007, the book was adapted into a film; controversy ensued over the use of Afghan boys in the rape scene.

After the publication of his novel, Hosseini took a leave of absence from the medical field to write a second book. *A Thousand Splendid Suns* was published in 2007 and focuses on the relationship between two Afghan wives with the same misogynistic husband; they live during the brutal times of the Taliban yet remain resilient.

Hosseini is married to Roya, an attorney, and has a son, Haris, and a daughter, Farah. They live in Northern California. Hosseini has been a volunteer for Paralyzed Vets of America and Aid the Afghan Children. In 2006, he became goodwill ambassador for the United Nations Refugee Agency.

DERBY PUBLIC LIBRARY
313 Elizabeth St.
Derby, CT 06418

The Story Behind the Story

With the destruction of the World Trade Center on September 11, 2001, Americans were faced with the unfamiliar reality of terrorist acts occurring in their own nation. Afghanistan was seen as a haven for some of the terrorists and their allies responsible for the attack, and the United States and others attempted retaliation. As the fight against terrorists continued and appeared increasingly complex, awareness of once overlooked or little-known places such as Afghanistan grew. By 2003, there had been published an increasing number of nonfiction books about Afghanistan, its recent history, and U.S. involvement there, but Khaled Hosseini's *The Kite Runner*, published that year, gained attention for providing a different perspective. In an interview with Riverhead Books, Hosseini describes what he hopes readers will get from his novel:

> I want them to see that the Afghan people existed before there was a war with the Soviets and before there was a Taliban. I want them to understand that the things we're seeing now in Afghanistan—the tribal chiefs vying for their own interests and the various ethnicities colliding with each other—have roots that go back several centuries. . . . I want readers to have a really good time reading this story. I want them to be touched by it because to me novel writing, first and foremost, is storytelling. . . . And I want people to simply remember Afghanistan. If the book is successful at all in sparking some dialogue on Afghanistan, and keeping it in the public consciousness, then I think it will have achieved a lot.

In addition, Hosseini showed in the novel the kinds of lives some Afghans had once they left their home country. Specifically, he wrote of the experience of those who came to California.

The Kite Runner grew in popularity, eventually spending more than two years on the *New York Times* bestseller list. As

DERBY PUBLIC LIBRARY
313 Elizabeth St.
Derby, CT 06418

Hosseini told afghanmagazine.com, "I get many letters and e-mails from readers who say how much more compassion they feel for Afghanistan and Afghans after reading this book—some even offering to help or donate money. We forget sometimes that fiction can be a powerful medium that way."

Hosseini has also related certain incidents from his life that inspired him to write his book. More specifically, he remembers a family cook he befriended when he was a young boy. Hosseini found out that the cook could not read or write, as prejudice against the Hazara left most uneducated, with no access to schooling. When Hosseini was in third grade, he took it upon himself to teach the cook, who was appreciative of the efforts. Another person from the author's childhood inspired and influenced the creation of the character Hassan. He was a Hazara boy who was a playmate of Hosseini and his friends. One day when Hosseini was about ten years old, he and his brother were told in crude terms by a man who worked for their family that he had raped the boy a number of times. Hosseini and his brother were too young to understand at first what the man was talking about. When they finally came to understand the nature of the man's act, they never told on him. The Hosseini boys feared the man, while also realizing that, even if they reported the crime, little or nothing would result.

Hosseini has explained that while he was inspired to create the central character of Hassan, the boy could not be the novel's protagonist. It is Amir whom Hosseini cast in that key role, since he is stricken with guilt, a conflicted figure who grows and changes. In this way, Hosseini added depth and complexity to his portrayal, addressing regret and the need for redemption and showing troubled relationships between brothers because of domineering fathers.

Since Hosseini himself immigrated to the United States before the great challenges facing Afghanistan in the 1980s and 1990s, he has been asked how he wrote certain parts of his novel so vividly. Afghans are storytellers, he has said, and he heard accounts from various Afghans in addition to doing extensive research. In 2007, after *The Kite Runner* was published, Hosseini, who had not been to Afghanistan for twenty-seven years, saw firsthand the destruction that had taken place. The stories he heard there were as brutal as the ones he had solicited earlier and had used to help write his book. Poverty had left its mark on the struggling nation. Despite this, Hosseini wrote in the *Guardian* afterwards, "I think of the strength of the Afghan people. I think of their humility. Their astonishing grace."

List of Characters

Amir, the narrator, is a Pashtun and a Sunni Muslim. As a boy, he lives with his father in an estate in Kabul, Afghanistan. He calls himself a coward, has a personality unlike his father's, and is haunted for years by an event from his childhood. He marries Soraya Taheri.

Baba is Amir's father and Sofia's husband. He is nicknamed Mr. Hurricane because of his size, strength, and power. He is one of the richest merchants in Kabul.

Sofia Akrami is Baba's wife and Amir's mother. A descendant of the royal family, she is beautiful, virtuous, and highly educated and teaches literature at a university. She is greatly admired and respected.

Rahim Khan is the best friend and business partner of Baba. He understands Amir and looks out for him.

Hassan is a servant in Baba's house, a Shi'a Muslim, and an ethnic Hazara; he is good friends with Amir. He is described as incapable of hurting anyone and is steadfastly loyal. He grows up as the son of Ali.

Ali is a servant in Baba's house, a Shi'a Muslim, and ethnic Hazara. He is a gentle man whose right leg is deformed and shrunken due to polio. He is often made fun of but does not seem affected by the jeers. Hassan is the joy of his life.

Sanaubar is Ali's wife, also Hazaran and a Shi'a Muslim. She is nineteen years younger than Ali, a first cousin, and "beautiful but notoriously unscrupulous."

Mahmood is an airline pilot and a friend of Baba's. He lives on an estate with his German wife and son, Assef.

Assef is the son of Mahmood. As a boy, Amir describes Assef as a sociopath. Assef is good looking, tall, and older than Amir and Hassan. He carries brass knuckles and is nicknamed the Ear Eater because of a fight he was once in.

Wali and **Kamal** are friends of Assef's and henchmen. They, too, are tall and older than Hassan and Amir.

Homayoun is Baba's second cousin. He studied engineering in France and had a house in Jalalabad. He has two wives, twin daughters, and two sons.

Fazila and **Karima** are the twin daughters of Homayoun, about five years younger than Amir. Amir cannot tell the two apart.

Shafiqa and **Nader** are cousins of Homayoun.

Faruq is Nader's brother.

Karim is a smuggler who helps people get out of Afghanistan after the Soviet invasion.

Toor, Karim's brother, is also a smuggler.

Aziz is a cousin of Karim's who has smuggled people as well.

Iqbal Taheri was a decorated general in Kabul who worked for the Ministry of Defense. His wife is Jamila, and Soraya is his daughter. He is distinguished looking and has great respect for Baba.

Jamila Taheri is Iqbal's wife. In Kabul she taught Farsi and history at a girls' high school. She has red hair, green eyes, and capped teeth. She is warm to Amir from the moment she meets him.

Soraya Taheri is the daughter of Iqbal and Jamila and the person Amir marries. Amir describes her as a beauty with black hair, walnut-brown eyes, and a nose that reminds him of a princess from old Persia. She is kind and empathic.

Sharif is Soraya's uncle from Virginia who works for the U.S. Immigration and Naturalization Service (INS) and has lived in the United States for more than twenty years. He also is a poet and is married to an American.

Farzana is Hassan's wife, a light-skinned Hazara who is quiet and courteous and who honors and admires Hassan.

Sohrab is the son of Hassan and Farzana. He is named after Hassan's favorite hero from the book *Shahnamah* and has a temperament similar to Hassan's.

Farid is a driver hired to bring Amir from Pakistan back to Afghanistan. He is lanky, dark, weather beaten, and twenty-nine years old but looks much older. He has two wives and five children and fought with his father against the Russians.

Wahid is Farid's older brother. He is welcoming and curious about Amir.

Maryam is Wahid's wife. She is accommodating and quiet and concerned about not having enough food for her children.

Zaman is the director of the orphanage in Karteh-Seh, a neighborhood in Kabul. He is short, thin, and balding.

Raymond Andrews works at the U.S. embassy in Islamabad. He is short and curt. His daughter has committed suicide. Initially Amir believes he lacks empathy, but he tries to help Amir.

Omar Faisal is the immigration lawyer in Islamabad that Raymond Andrews recommends to Amir. Faisal is chubby, disorganized, and prone to laughter and apologies. He sympathizes with Amir's plight in trying to adopt Sohrab.

Summary and Analysis

Chapter one is dated December 2001 but opens by mentioning events from 1975, when the narrator, relating the story in the first person, was twelve years old; the events still haunt him, entail "unatoned sins," and made him who he is today. The narrator was reminded anew of the fateful events when his friend Rahim Khan called him, asking him to come see him in Pakistan. The narrator was then living in San Francisco and after the phone call went outside. As he observes kites in the sky, he mentions Hassan, "the harelipped kite runner" and mentions the names of others not yet familiar to the reader.

In **chapter two**, the narrator recalls his childhood. He and his friend Hassan would play in the poplar trees, and the narrator would press Hassan to use his slingshot against the neighbor's dog in addition to other pranks. Later, when Ali (whom the narrator describes as Hassan's father) reprimands the boys, Hassan does not blame his friend for prodding him. The narrator explains that the poplar trees line the driveway leading to the luxurious estate of his father, Baba, in a new and rich neighborhood in the northern part of Kabul, the capital of Afghanistan. The narrator describes photographs found there, of a grandfather hunting with a king; of a beautiful mother; of Rahim Khan, Baba's best friend and business partner.

In contrast to Amir's comfortable existence, Hassan and Ali are servants and their home is "a modest little mud hut." More comparisons are made. The narrator's mother died giving birth to him, and Hassan, born a year later, also lost his mother, Sanaubar, less than a week after he was born. She ran off with traveling singers and dancers, an action considered a great disgrace.

Sanaubar was beautiful and unscrupulous, and most saw her as an odd match for Ali. Ali, like Hassan, has a physical disability. Ali has a bad limp, due to the effects of polio. He is made fun of for his gait and also for being a Hazara. The narrator explains that, by chance, after years of not knowing the history of the Hazaras, he read about their heritage and how his people, the Pashtuns, had abused and killed the Hazaras partially because they adopted the Shi'a and not the Sunni branch of Islam.

The two boys, left without mothers, were nursed by the same woman Baba hired and are told that there is a kinship between them as a result. The narrator's first word was *Baba*; Hassan's was *Amir*, the narrator's name, which is significant to what transpired later in 1975.

Additional contrasts are established in **chapter three.** It focuses on Baba and his relationship to his son, which differs from the descriptions of Ali and Hassan in the previous chapter. The chapter opens with Amir saying that legend states that Baba once wrestled a black bear. Whether the story is true or not, and there are indications that it is, Baba is a formidable figure—tall, big, strong, and with a powerful personality.

When Amir is five or six, his father decides to design and finance the building of an orphanage. Baba has no experience with architecture yet proves he can design it. The day before the orphanage is to open, Baba says he and his son and Hassan should go to a picnic at a lake. Yet Amir, jealous of the closeness between Baba and Hassan, invents a reason why Hassan cannot go. At the lake, Baba is wrapped up in preparing his speech for the orphanage's opening and pays little attention to his son. The next day, at the orphanage, Baba makes a grand speech that impresses the crowd. Amir is proud of his father's success and notes that, while people frequently seemed to doubt his father, Baba would prove them wrong. People had once scoffed about his career and his marriage prospects, for example, but he had become a wealthy businessman and married a highly respected and beautiful woman.

Amir reveals that although Baba usually got what he wanted in life, that was not the case when it came to his son. Amir admits he fears his father and dislikes him a little as well. Baba tries to bring up Amir in his own image, but that proves challenging. When the boy questions how his father can drink alcohol, when his teacher had told him that doing so is a sin, Baba gives Amir his own nonconformist view and tells his son not to listen to the religious men, whom he calls "self-righteous monkeys." He tells him that there is only one sin, the sin of theft, and that all sins are versions of that. As Amir struggles to understand, he sees his father get frustrated. He thinks of how his father must hate him, too, since, after all, he was responsible for killing the man's wife, who hemorrhaged after giving birth to Amir.

The differences between father and son are stark. Amir envelops himself in books, many of which were his mother's, and memorizes poetry. Baba tries in vain to get his son to excel at sports, then to at least be interested in watching sports. He is disturbed after Amir is upset by a brutal sporting event. Later, Amir strains to overhear his father talking to Rahim. The young boy hears how Baba is distressed that his son is so unlike him. Baba says he sees his son never standing up for himself, a dangerous situation in his view, since he could potentially grow into a man unable to stand up for anything. Baba's words will prove prophetic. Rahim tries to steer Baba's thinking in a more positive direction but cannot sway him.

Chapter four begins with descriptions of similarities in characters' relationships. Amir reveals that Ali actually was orphaned at a young age and that Baba's father took Ali in. Ali and Baba, then, became playmates when they were very young. Their relationship appears similar to that of Amir and Hassan's. Baba would encourage Ali to get into trouble, just as Amir does with Hassan. As much as Baba talks of the fun he had with Ali, he never refers to Ali as his friend, just as Amir never thought of Hassan as his friend. Amir seems to accept society's divisions and says nothing can be done about the fact that he is a Pashtun and a Sunni and that Hassan is not.

Amir recalls how he and Hassan had great fun together for much of their early years. Differences emerge, though, as Hassan is the diligent servant who gets up early and prepares everything for Amir, while Amir is the one who sleeps late and complains. When Amir returns from school at the end of the day, often he reads Hassan stories and at times plays tricks on him, giving Hassan the exact opposite definitions of words he does not know. While Hassan will never be sent to school and will remain illiterate, he actually is better at comprehending than Amir is and so he intimidates Amir. Hassan's favorite story is an ancient tale in which a father kills his rival, not realizing that the rival is in fact his son. Hassan wells up with tears because of the story, and Amir wonders if Hassan feels empathy for the father or the son; Amir believes Hassan should not feel bad for the father, since all fathers seem to want to kill their sons.

One day, after receiving Hassan's encouragement, Amir writes his own story. The young boy is disappointed, though, when he is done writing and his father is uninterested in reading his work. But Rahim says he would be delighted to read it and gives Amir praise and encouragement. When Amir rushes to read the story to Hassan, he, too, praises it, although he points out a plot problem. Amir, insulted, tries to offer an excuse for it but is interrupted.

Amir was interrupted, we learn in **chapter five**, by the sound of gunfire outside. The boys run to Ali for protection, and he holds Hassan tight, provoking Amir's envy. They later learn that the government has been overthrown; Afghanistan would no longer have a king. Men on the radio talk of a republic, but the boys do not understand what is being discussed. Hassan worries that he will be sent away, but Amir assures him that will not happen.

The two friends go to climb their favorite pomegranate tree but on the way are confronted by three other boys, Assef, Wali, and Kamal. Assef is a troublemaker who taunts Hassan's father more than the others in their neighborhood do. Assef picks on Hassan and Amir and brags that his father knows Daoud Khan, the man who has unseated the king. The bully says he plans to tell the new ruler that Afghanistan should only be for Pashtuns, not for Hazaras like Hassan.

Amir tries to stand up to Assef, but Assef will not relent nor let the boys by. Assef takes out his brass knuckles and chastises

Amir for being friends with a Hazara. Amir at first thinks that Hassan is not his friend but then realizes he is, or maybe even more like a brother. Still Hassan is someone Amir does not play with if other friends are present.

Before Assef can take a swing at Amir, Hassan steps in, aiming his loaded slingshot directly at Assef's eye. Assef backs down but warns the two that they will resume their fight another time. Amir and Hassan are shaken.

Amir states that, for the next few years, people in Afghanistan are hopeful. The country is a republic and has a president. People look to development and improvement, even though life goes on relatively unchanged. In the winter of 1974, Baba gives Hassan an unusual birthday present. Baba introduces Hassan to a plastic surgeon who will fix Hassan's harelip. The surgery goes well, and Amir says that by the following winter only a slight scar is left; ironically, that is the last winter that Hassan smiled.

What winter means to a young boy in Kabul is described in **chapter six**. Amir writes that school is closed for the icy season for three months. Winter also is kite time in Kabul, and kite flying, which Amir relishes, brings the boys closer together.

The pinnacle of the kite-flying season is the tournament. Amir relates the tournament rules. All kite fighters have an assistant. The goal is to take down the other kites using tricks and glass-enhanced kite string until yours is the last kite flying. In addition, all kite fighters vie for the fallen kites. Each time a kite falls, hordes of kids run through the streets chasing after it as spectators cheer.

Hassan displays a keen sense for where a kite will land. Amir recalls following him in one such chase. As they wait for the kite to fall, Amir asks Hassan how he knows the kite will fall there. Hassan says he would sooner eat dirt than lie to Amir, and Amir is taken by his loyalty. Hassan assures him of his words but then asks Amir if he would ever actually ask Hassan to eat dirt. Amir feels his answer is forced but that Hassan's affirmation of his loyalty was not. Amir portrays his friend as someone who always means everything he says and who also thinks others can be taken at their word.

Amir relates that the winter of 1975 would be the last time he would see Hassan run for a kite. That winter many districts decide to join together to hold one tournament, a development that provokes great excitement. The night before the contest, Baba tells Amir he thinks Amir will win it. With that assurance, Amir promises himself he will. He spends time that evening playing cards with Hassan.

The boys talk of Afghanistan eventually getting television sets. Amir wonders why Hassan would be content to live in his meager home his whole life, and Hassan reads his friends's mind, which, Amir notes, is not unusual. Hassan says he likes where he lives—it is home.

Chapter seven opens on the morning of the contest. Hassan tells Amir his dream from the night before, in which Amir jumped into a lake that supposedly had a monster in it and Hassan jumped in after him. Other people were present, watching them from shore and then clapping when they realized that there really was no monster. When Hassan asks Amir what the dream means, Amir, nervous over the impending kite contest, is cross with him.

The boys head outside, where Baba, Rahim, and a large crowd have gathered to watch the tournament. Amir tells Hassan maybe he will not fly his kite after all, but Hassan, who immediately understands that Amir is afraid, tells him not to worry, that there is no monster; he gets Amir to calm down and consent to competing in the contest.

About one hundred kites are entered in the tournament. Amir is concerned about his father watching him, but he stays in the contest as many of the kites fall. Eventually, two kites are left, one of which is Amir's, and tension builds as the crowd calls for the last kite to be cut.

Amir cuts the last kite down, and he and Hassan laugh and weep in victory. Seeing Amir's father so proud of him was the happiest moment of the boy's life to that point. Hassan rushes off to get the fallen kite and calls back to Amir that he *will* get it—"For you a thousand times over!" As Amir prepares to leave with his winning kite, he imagines how wonderful it will feel when he goes home, a hero.

When Hassan does not return, Amir searches for him. As Amir looks, people in the streets are congratulating him. He asks a boy if he has seen Hassan. The boy makes fun of Hassan for being a Hazara then points to where he has gone. Amir heads off in that direction, asking one of the many merchants if he has seen Hassan. This man, too, remarks on what he sees as the deservedly low status of the Hazara, then also reveals the place where he thinks Hassan has gone.

When Amir turns a corner and looks down an alley, he sees Hassan holding the kite, cornered by Assef, Kamal, and Wali. Assef says he will take the kite, but Hassan declares that Amir deserves it. Assef mocks Hassan for being so loyal and points out how Amir is not really Hassan's friend. With that, Hassan throws a rock at Assef and the three boys attack him. Shutting his eyes, Amir is flooded with various thoughts—of how he and Hassan were breast-fed by the same woman; of how a fortune teller had once seen something so distressing in Hassan's future that he would not reveal it; of a dream Amir had in which he was lost in a blinding snowstorm but saved by a person with a familiar shape.

Amir sees Assef as he prepares to rape Hassan while the other boys hold him down. Amir sees Hassan's resigned expression and thinks of the same look on the sheep that get slaughtered as part of a religious ritual; they look as if they are dying for a higher cause. Rather than help, Amir runs away. When he later sees Assef and the two other boys pass by laughing, Amir goes back to search for Hassan. The beaten Hassan looks as if he might collapse but hands Amir the kite. Pretending he does not know what has happened, Amir wonders if Hassan realizes that his friend actually knows of the rape. Hassan attempts to speak but limps away. Amir goes home to the open arms of his smiling father, proud of his victorious son.

Chapter eight conveys how various relationships have changed. Hassan does his chores but the rest of the time wants to stay in bed. Ali asks Amir what is wrong, but Amir only snaps at Ali. Amir and Baba's relations, though, are strong. Baba happily does anything Amir asks. Amir suggests they go to Jalalabad but is disconcerted when Baba says Hassan should come too; Amir says Hassan is sick and cannot come.

Baba tells his second cousin, Homayoun, about their trip, and the cousin invites them to his home in Jalalabad, asking many others as well. The trip is lengthy, and on the way Baba brags about how Amir won the contest, but Amir notices that Rahim remains silent and has an odd look on his face. Even though the others cheer Amir, he feels empty, stating that that night he became an insomniac.

For the duration of the winter, Amir is happy when Baba is home but spends the rest of the time in his room. Hassan tries to revive their friendship, but Amir cannot bear to be with him. In spring, when Amir and Baba are enjoying planting tulip bulbs together, Amir asks if maybe they should get new servants, and Baba is shocked and angered to hear such a suggestion. Their relationship cools.

School starts again, and after class one day Amir asks Hassan to come outside with him so he can read him a story. Hassan is excited to go. On the hill Amir asks Hassan what he would do if he hit him with a pomegranate that has fallen to the ground. The color drains from Hassan's face. Amir hits him with a pomegranate, which breaks on his chest. Amir yells at Hassan to hit him back and throws more pomegranates, hoping Hassan will retaliate and give Amir the punishment he thinks he deserves. Hassan, though, will not be provoked to violence and instead takes a piece of pomegranate, smashes it against his own forehead, and walks away, leaving Amir, who cries alone.

For Amir's thirteenth birthday, Baba throws an extravagant party and invites more than four hundred guests. Baba makes sure Amir properly greets all the guests, one of whom, it turns out, is Assef. He arrives with his parents, appearing to be the more powerful one, as they remain silent while he chats and flatters Baba. When Amir finally leaves the party, he is disgusted by the grinning, evil bully. Amir opens the present Assef said he picked himself for Amir, a biography of Hitler, a man Assef had said he admired the first time he had cornered Amir and Hassan. Amir throws the book into the weeds.

Wishing the party was over, Amir sits on the ground. He hears a voice, it is Rahim Khan's. The friend raises his drink in honor of Amir and proceeds to tell him a story of how, when Rahim was a young man, he had fallen in love with the daughter of a servant who was a Hazara. The two planned a marvelous wedding, but when Rahim told his parents his plans, his mother fainted and his father had the girl and her family sent away. Rahim tells Amir the world is very strong and always wins but that, nonetheless, the matter probably worked out for the best.

Rahim also tells Amir he can confide in him whenever he wants, and Amir almost confesses to him what happened the day of the kite contest but decides he cannot, since such an admission would only cause Rahim to hate him.

Rahim gives Amir his birthday present, a leather-covered notebook for his stories, a perfect gift for the young teenager. Fireworks start to light up the grounds of the estate, and the two join the guests to watch them. In between the flashes of the fireworks, Amir sees Hassan serving drinks to Assef and Wali; Assef grins and kneads his knuckles into Hassan's chest. Amir is thankful when darkness comes again, so he does not have to see the interaction, reminiscent of the time he closed his eyes rather than watch or intervene as Assef assaulted Hassan on the day of the contest.

Chapter nine opens the next day; Amir unwraps and piles the presents from his guests. He is uninterested, believing the only reason his father had thrown him such an extravagant party was because Amir had won the kite tournament. He thinks of Rahim's story, and Amir decides he or Hassan "had to go." Amir passes Ali and Hassan cleaning up from the party, and Ali gives Amir his present, a new copy of the book Amir had read with Hassan so many times, *Shahnamah*. The book is beautiful, and, although Ali says it is not worthy of Amir, Amir thinks that he, instead, is not worthy of the book.

The next morning, Amir takes the watch his father gave him and some of his birthday money and puts it under Hassan's mattress. Then, Amir goes to his father and tells what he hopes will "be the last in a long line of shameful lies." When Ali and

Hassan return, Baba goes to them and then calls Amir to his office. Ali and Hassan later enter, with eyes red from crying, and when Baba asks Hassan whether he stole the money and watch, Hassan says he did. Amir is shocked that Hassan is still willing to make such a sacrifice for him. Amir finally realizes that Hassan knows that Amir had witnessed his sexual assault in the alley. Amir feels great love for his friend and wants to tell them all he is guilty, but a part of him is glad that his pain is about to end, as Ali and Hassan will be forced to leave the household and Amir will be free of the guilt associated with his friend's presence.

Instead, Amir is shocked again when Baba says he forgives Hassan. Ali, though, says that he and Hassan must leave. Amir sees from Ali's face that Hassan has told him the whole story of what happened in the alley the day of the contest. Baba cries and sobs, but the two leave. Amir is sorry, but he does not confess.

In **chapter ten**, it is March 1981; Amir, now eighteen, and his father are in the back of an old truck along with several other people. They are being smuggled out of Kabul, which has become overrun with Russian soldiers and tanks. A driver, Karim, is taking them to Jalalabad, and from there his brother, Toor, will drive them into Pakistan. Baba apologizes for the fact that his son is carsick. When the truck pulls over, Amir gets sick as fighter aircraft fly overhead.

At a checkpoint, an Afghan soldier and a Russian soldier inspect the vehicle and its passengers. The Russian wants some time alone with the young woman in the truck. She bursts into tears. Her husband pleads with Karim to dissuade the soldier. Then Baba jumps in to protect the woman as well. The Russian says he will shoot him, but Baba says he will proudly take a thousand bullets. When Amir tries to get Baba to back down, Baba asks if he has not taught his son anything after all. A bullet is heard, but it turns out to be from another soldier's gun. This soldier calms the Russian who had his gun pointed at Baba, and the travelers are allowed to resume their journey.

In Jalalabad, the travelers are brought to a house. There Karim announces that Toor's truck has unfortunately not been working since the previous week. The travelers are angry, realizing that Karim took their money, even though he knew there was no ready transportation available. Baba lunges at the man and nearly chokes him to death, halting only because the young woman from the truck pleads for him to stop.

The group is ushered into a dark rat-infested basement where others are waiting as well. Among the group are Kamal, Assef's friend, and Kamal's father. The father tells of the tragedy that has beset his family; Kamal is left staring and speechless.

The Afghans learn that they can get a ride in a tanker truck that Karim's cousin, Aziz, owns and will drive. Once in the truck, Amir describes the stench and horrible feeling of not being able to breathe; his father whispers for him to divert his thoughts to something more pleasant, and he recalls kite flying with Hassan. Eventually the travelers make it to Pakistan. Amir is grateful, although he writes that he feels bad for his father, who is left with only a disappointing son and two suitcases. They hear a wailing. It is Kamal's father. He holds his son, who is lifeless. Quickly the father reaches for Karim's gun and kills himself.

Chapter eleven describes Amir and Baba's experiences in Fremont, California, in the 1980s. One Sunday in the spring of 1983, Baba becomes furious in a little grocery store when he is asked for identification after writing a check. Oranges are strewn across the floor, a magazine rack is overturned, a jar of beef jerky is broken. Amir apologizes for his father and says they will certainly pay for everything. He thinks of how in Afghanistan there are no checks and identification involved when making purchases. Baba has been in the United States for a year and a half and is still adjusting. He misses his home and now, working in a gas station, has blackened, chipped fingernails. Feeling sorry for Baba, Amir says they could go back to Peshawar, where Baba was happier, but Baba says it was not the right place for his son, that they have come to California instead.

In 1983, Amir, twenty years old, graduates from high school. Baba takes him out to dinner and then to a bar where Baba assembles a party of several other patrons, buying them drinks and songs on the jukebox. Afterward, Baba gives Amir an old Ford Grand Torino. Amir is stunned and touched. They take it for a test ride, and, when they return home, Baba says he wishes Hassan could have joined them for their celebration. Amir feels as if he is being choked.

The next day Amir announces he will start junior college and be an English major. His father cannot understand such a decision, but Amir promises himself he will not give in. Amir is still amazed at the vastness of the United States and sees it as "Someplace with no ghosts, no memories, and no sins."

Amir describes their weekend routine in the summer of 1984. They scavenge at garage sales on Saturday and then on Sunday resell their findings at a profit at the San Jose flea market, where many other Afghan families do the same. There is Afghan music, tea, political discussions, and gossip. Baba saunters amid people he knew from Kabul. On one such morning, Baba introduces Amir to Iqbal Taheri, who had been a decorated general in Kabul, and the general's daughter, Soraya. Amir is struck by her beauty. Later Amir asks Baba about a story that has been circulating about her. Something happened between her and a man, Baba says, and ever since, no suitors have appeared. Baba warns his son that what can happen in just a single day can affect a lifetime. Later that night, Amir thinks not of Hassan but of Soraya and how she had met his glance.

Amir describes in **chapter twelve** his continuing obsession with Soraya. Months go by before Amir actually speaks to her. Afghans have long established and rigid notions of how young unmarried men and women are to interact, so Amir knows he must be respectful. When he speaks to Soraya, she mentions that she knows that Amir writes, and he finds himself saying he might bring her something of his to read one day. Soraya's mother appears and introduces herself. In her eyes, Amir sees hope and thinks of how Soraya has not had any suitors, seemingly because of the gossip that has spread about her.

For weeks Amir waits until the general leaves the Taheri's stall so he can talk to Soraya, whose mother is sometimes there as well. Soraya tells him that she is in school and studying to be a teacher. She relates how she had taught a family servant to read and write and how proud she had been. The story reminds Amir of how he had not only not helped Hassan learn how to read but had taken pleasure in telling him the wrong meaning of words. On one visit with Soraya, Amir gives her one of his stories, but her father arrives, takes the pages from her hand, and throws them in the trash.

Life takes another turn for Amir and Baba, when they find out that Baba has advanced, inoperable cancer. A doctor tells them that Baba could get chemotherapy, although that would only address Baba's symptoms, not cure him. Baba refuses the treatment and smokes all the way home from the doctor's office. Later, when Amir wells up with tears and asks what will become of him without his father, Baba snaps back that he is a grown man, that "All those years, that's what I was trying to teach you, how to never have to ask that question." Baba also insists that Amir not tell anyone about the cancer.

Despite his deteriorating health, Baba keeps up the routine of going to garage sales and the flea market on weekends. Then one day at the flea market, Baba falls to the ground in the grips of a seizure.

At the hospital, a doctor tells Amir that Baba's cancer has spread to his brain. The next morning, Baba gets a stream of visitors, including the Taheri family. The general says he will do anything for Baba, just as he would for a brother, and Amir recalls when Baba had told him that Pashtuns are hardheaded and overly proud but that they can be relied on when help is needed. This loyalty contrasts with Amir's failure to help his friend during the assault. When the general kindly asks Amir what he needs as well, Amir cannot hold back his tears and rushes out of the room. In the hallway, Soraya comes to comfort him, and he tells her how much he appreciates her being there.

Two days later, Baba is out of the hospital. Amir asks him if he has the strength to do him a favor, to go and ask the general if Amir can marry his daughter. The next day, Amir brings Baba to the Taheri's home and waits for his phone call. Baba calls Amir and says that all has gone well and that Soraya wants to talk to Amir. The young woman tells Amir that when she was eighteen she ran away with a man and lived with him for almost a month. She says it was a foolish thing to do, that the man was doing drugs, and that once her father found her, he convinced her to return home. Soraya starts to cry as she tells Amir that, when she got home, she learned that her mother had had a stroke resulting in the paralysis of one side of her face, a development that left Soraya with deep feelings of guilt.

Soraya asks if the story bothers Amir, and he admits that it does. He nonetheless realizes that he is not beyond reproach in his conduct either, stating "How could I, of all people, chastise someone for their past?" For a moment he almost tells her what happened with Hassan, but he hesitates and thinks how in many ways Soraya is probably a better person than he is.

The next evening, as described in **chapter thirteen**, Amir and Baba go to the Taheri home to celebrate the engagement. Along with many guests, they follow the celebratory Afghan customs. While engagements usually last a few months, because Baba is so sick, the families decide the wedding should take place soon.

At the wedding, many traditions are again followed. The bride and groom dress in green, the color of Islam but also symbolic of spring. Part of the Koran is read, an uncle reads a poem, the couple and a procession head toward the stage. Amir wishes Rahim was in attendance and wonders if Hassan is married. The ideas stand in contrast to Baba's sentiments at Amir's graduation, when Baba had wished Hassan could be there also.

Once married, Soraya decides she should move into Amir and Baba's apartment, and she lovingly takes care of Baba as his health declines. One night Baba admits to Amir that he has shown Soraya Amir's stories and, when she reveals how impressed she is with his talent, Amir leaves the room and cries.

A month after the wedding, Baba dies in his sleep. For the funeral, the mosque is filled. Between rounds of prayers, mourners voice their thoughts and feelings about Baba to Amir. He realizes how much of his life has been defined by his role as Baba's son and is terrified of having to find his own way. After the mourners leave, the general asks Amir how he is doing, but he must walk away before his tears start. He finds Soraya and lets his tears freely flow.

Amir learns more about his in-laws. The general can be heartless and petty, does not sleep with his wife, and has never held a job in the United States. He believes Afghanistan will be freed and that he will work there again. His wife was once a famous singer in Kabul, but when they were married her husband made her promise she would never sing in public again. She is enchanted by Amir, especially because he has married her daughter.

At a family wedding, Amir sees further examples of how sexist Afghan society is when someone makes a comment about his wife's lack of virtues. Soraya is pushed to tears and rails against the different rules for men and women and how her father was ready to kill the man she ran off with as well as himself when he arrived to take his eighteen-year-old daughter back home. She reveals how once she was home her father made her cut off her hair. Amir calms her, and she remarks that he is vastly different from other Afghan men. He thinks to himself it might be because he had only grown up with men and with a father who did not adhere to many societal rules. Mostly he thinks that Soraya's running off with a man in the past does not bother him because he regrets part of his former conduct as well.

Amir and Soraya move into an apartment, and Amir is accepted at San Jose State. He takes a job as a security guard and begins writing his first novel during the hours at work when there is little to do. His wife enrolls at the university the following year, intent on becoming a teacher even though this is against her father's wishes.

In the summer of 1988, the Soviets are on the brink of withdrawing from Afghanistan, and Amir had finished his novel about a father and son in Kabul. Not long after, he finds an agent who finds him a publisher. In 1989, war still rages in Afghanistan. Amir and his wife try to conceive a child and are frustrated by their lack of success. After numerous tests and various treatments, the doctor tells them they could consider adoption, but Soraya wants her own baby. Soraya's father explains that adoption is not a feasible option for Afghans, since to them lineage is of great importance. Amir thinks the couple's inability to have a child may be a form of punishment for his past. He and Soraya use the advance from Amir's second novel to buy a house. Amir continues to feel empty and saddened by their childless state.

In **chapter fourteen**, the narrative shifts to June 2001. Amir hangs up the telephone; his wife says he looks pale, and she stops grading the papers from the school where she has been teaching for the last six years. Amir tells her he must go to Pakistan because Rahim Khan is very sick.

Taking a solitary walk, Amir thinks of Rahim's comment on the telephone: "There is a way to be good again." Amir realizes Rahim knows the story of what happened between Amir and Hassan.

Soraya's parents plan to stay with her while Amir is gone. The family dynamic has changed somewhat. The general had broken his hip two years earlier and has suffered numerous serious consequences. He is frail and has also become warmer toward his daughter.

At night, Amir recalls how he and his wife had been so hopeful about having a child and how they both try not to think about it now. In his dreams, he sees Hassan running off to retrieve the last fallen kite, calling, "For you, a thousand times over!" A week later, Amir is on a plane to Pakistan.

During the taxi ride to Rahim's home, recounted in **chapter fifteen**, Amir remembers saying good-bye to Rahim in 1981 before Amir and his father left Kabul. After that, Rahim and Baba would phone each other four or five times a year, and sometimes Amir would speak to Rahim then as well.

When Amir arrives at Rahim's place, he finds Rahim looking emaciated. Amir fills him in on his life and tells him he now has published four novels. He asks Rahim what it has been like under the Taliban, and Rahim reports that it is even worse than what has been reported. Rahim had lived in Baba's house since 1981, because Baba remained hopeful that Afghanistan would regain its former stability. But Rahim tells of the grim realities that had beset the nation from 1992 to 1996, when different factions of the Northern Alliance assumed control of various sections of Kabul. People for the most part stayed in their homes, hoping they would not be hit by explosive devices. Part of the collateral damage was the orphanage Baba had painstakingly built. When the Taliban assumed power and ousted the alliance, Afghanis were thrilled and hopeful. Peace was established but at a price.

Rahim reveals that he will probably die before the end of the summer. He also reveals that while he lived in Baba's house, Hassan was there as well. Amir is struck by the news and feels strangled with guilt again at the thought of Hassan. Rahim knows he has broached a sensitive subject, but he tells Amir he needs him to do something for him but that first he must tell Amir about Hassan.

In **chapter sixteen**, Rahim relates how he had been lonely in Kabul and suffering from arthritis; when he heard the news of Baba's death, he felt even more alone, so in 1986 he sought out Hassan, who was living with his pregnant wife, Farzana. Rahim finds out from Hassan that Ali had been killed by a land mine two years before.

Rahim asks Hassan if he will come and live with him, saying that he will pay him well to help him take care of the house. Hassan and his wife kindly decline the offer, though. Then Hassan asks Rahim for news of Amir and Baba. Rahim tells the little that he knows, and when he tells Hassan that Baba has died, Hassan cries the entire evening.

The next morning Hassan says he and his wife have decided to move to Kabul with Rahim. At the house, they do repairs, clean, cook, and garden. In the fall, the couple's child arrives stillborn, but in early 1990 Farzana is pregnant again. That same year a toothless, hungry woman with slashes across her face arrives at the front gates and collapses. When she comes to, she asks for Hassan, cries when she sees him smile, says she remembers how he smiled when he was first born and that Allah should forgive her for not having wanted to hold him. Hassan realizes this is Sanaubar, his mother, and rushes out.

When he returns, he tells Sanaubar she is home with her family now. He and his wife nurse her back to health. She works often in the garden with Hassan, talking happily, and that winter helps deliver the couple's son and becomes thoroughly absorbed with his care. The boy, Sohrab, adores his aging grandmother, who dies in her sleep when the child is four.

Hassan, who had learned to read and write from a teacher he befriended, in turn teaches his son to read and write, insisting that he not grow up illiterate. In 1996, when the Taliban brought new hope by ending the years of factional fighting, Hassan is in fear. Two years later, the Taliban massacre Hazaras in Mazar-i-Sharif, a city in northern Afghanistan.

In **chapter seventeen** Amir asks if Hassan is still at Baba's house; in response, Rahim hands him an envelope. Inside is a photograph of Hassan and his son. Hassan looks self-assured and happy. Also in the envelope is a letter to Amir from Hassan. He lovingly wishes Amir well. He says he has told his wife and son stories of the fun they had growing up together. His feelings for Amir starkly contrast the way Amir has deliberately attempted to push Hassan out of his life and is still pained when Hassan's name is mentioned.

Hassan also relates that the Afghanistan they grew up in is gone forever. He writes of the killings and the other horrors perpetrated by the Taliban. Despite the threat of violence, there are still places from their childhood that Hassan explores with his son. Unable to have children, Amir and his wife have missed out on experiencing similar joys. Hassan also relates that he is teaching his son to read and write, so he will not "grow up stupid like his father." Again, Hassan is shown to have no animosity, no bitterness about not having had the opportunity to learn how to read and write earlier in his life.

When Amir finishes the letter and asks Rahim about Hassan, Rahim tells him that, a month after he left Hassan, he learned that Taliban officials took note of Baba's spacious house, accused Hassan of living in it as if it was his own, and told him they were moving in. When Hassan protested, they shot him and then his wife.

Rahim says that Hassan's son is in an orphanage and that Amir must go to Kabul to get him; Rahim says he knows an American couple in Peshawar that will take the boy in. But

Amir vehemently protests, saying he could not possibly go to such a dangerous place. Rahim asserts various reasons Amir should go and then, finally, tells him there is another reason, that Hassan was actually Baba's, not Ali's, son. Hassan was never told of his actual parentage. The fact had to be kept secret to save Baba's reputation. Amir is livid at the revelation and storms out.

Amir is in a samovar house getting a cup of tea in **chapter eighteen**. He wonders how he had not noticed all the clues that suggested that Hassan was his half-brother. He wonders how his father could have lied to him and Hassan, especially since Baba had told him that the only sin is theft and that lying is stealing the truth from others. His father had dishonored Ali as well. Amir once had such a strong vision of his father that no longer seems to apply.

Amir also realizes that he is more like his father than he had previously thought. Each had betrayed the person who was most loyal to him. Rahim was asking Amir to find Hassan's son to make up not only for Amir's own sins but his father's as well. Amir thinks of how different Hassan and Ali's lives could have been if Amir had not betrayed them. Maybe Baba would have brought them to the United States; they would still be alive. Amir heads back to Rahim's apartment and thinks how his father had not lied about one thing, that someone else always did Amir's fighting for him. Back at the apartment, Amir tells Rahim he will go to Kabul.

Farid is the young driver who is to get Amir into Afghanistan, as described in **chapter nineteen**. He looks much older than his actual age, fought with his father against the Russians, and had some of his toes and three fingers severed by a land mine. For the trip, Amir is dressed like Farid, and Rahim has even gotten Amir a fake beard to avoid drawing the attentions of the Taliban. Once Farid drives them across the border, Amir sees intense poverty and feels like a stranger in his own country. Farid is hostile toward him, and Amir asks why. The man tells him his assumptions about Amir and his former life—that he never really lived in the true Afghanistan but in a big house where there were servants and nice parties. He says

Amir probably has only come to sell his father's land and take the money back to the United States.

In Jalalabad, the two go to the dilapidated house of Farid's brother, Wahid, where they are to spend the night. Wahid asks Amir what he does in the United States, and when Amir says he is a writer, Wahid asks if he writes about Afghanistan. Thinking about what he actually writes, Amir becomes embarrassed. When Wahid asks Amir why he is in Afghanistan, Farid suggests that Amir is like all the others, just coming to sell his family's land. Wahid yells at his brother, angry that Farid is being so disrespectful.

Amir is frank, explaining that he is looking for a boy who is the son of his illegitimate brother. Wahid is impressed by Amir. Wahid's wife, Maryam, and her mother bring food for the two travelers, and Amir notices that the couple's three young boys are watching him. He believes they are fascinated by his watch and gives it to them.

That night Farid says he wished Amir had told him why he was going to Afghanistan. He says that maybe he will help Amir find the boy. Amir sleeps and dreams of Hassan on the ground ready to be assassinated. After the rifle shot, Amir sees that he is the man holding the gun. He wakes up horrified at the disturbing image.

Amir goes outside and feels a reconnection with the land. He hears bits of conversation between Wahid and his wife and realizes that the family has little food, that the boys had not been staring at his watch but at his food. Early the next morning, he leaves money under a mattress, just as he had done years earlier but this time with entirely honorable intentions.

In **chapter twenty**, Farid and Amir are traveling, from Jalalabad to Kabul. Farid, having learned of Amir's mission to locate Hassan's son, is more talkative. On the way, Amir sees the devastated landscape, and when they reach Kabul he is shocked, even though Farid had already warned him of the extreme changes. Many structures have been reduced to rubble; what is left are dilapidated buildings damaged from shelling. Beggars, many of them children, fill the streets. Trees have been cut down for firewood.

Amir asks Farid if they can walk around for a while. Members of the Taliban, visibly armed, drive by, and Amir stares at the men and is shaken by their presence. Farid tells him that he must never stare at the Taliban, and an old beggar on the street echoes Farid's warning, as members of the Taliban are easily provoked and need little or no reason to become violent. By chance, Amir learns that the beggar taught at the same university at which his mother was a professor and, in fact, that he knew her. Amir pleads with him to tell as much as he can about his mother, since his father only spoke of her broadly, never in detail. The man tells Amir he ate almond cake with her and that she was anxious about her happiness.

When Amir asks the man if he can tell him anything else, the man replies that he will think about it and tells Amir he should come back and find him again to check if he has remembered anything else. Amir has been in Pakistan and Afghanistan for only a short time and already feels closer to his mother, confused and angry at his father and Rahim for keeping the secret about Hassan, and distressed to find his childhood homeland devastated. So much has been altered, and his quest is far from over.

The orphanage is in one of the areas of Kabul most devastated by the war. A short, thin man opens the orphanage door to Amir and Farid but only lets them in after he hears them pleading. This man is Zaman, the director of the orphanage, and he tells them what grim conditions the children live in, since the orphanage is an unheated, overcrowded warehouse with no clean water and a rapidly diminishing food supply. Zaman admits that, out of desperation, when a Taliban official comes every once in a while and brings money and sometimes asks to take a girl, he turns over the child. Farid leaps at the man and starts strangling him, stopping only because it upsets some nearby children.

Zaman explains that he has given so much to these children and that he is broke and desperate. Besides, he insists, the official will only take more children if Zaman denies him one. Zaman says they can find the official who has taken Sohrab by going to Ghazi Stadium the next day.

In **chapter twenty-one**, Amir and Farid head to Ghazi Stadium. On the way, they pass a restaurant where Baba used to take Amir. A young man's dead body hangs from a rope there, and no one seems to notice.

Farid drives into Amir's old neighborhood, which, Amir is surprised to see, is not as altered as other parts of the capital. Farid explains that this is because the area is home to the Taliban's main supporters—Arabs, Chechens, and Pakistanis— who are running what passes for the nation's government. Amir sees his father's house. He remembers being with Hassan in the yard, imagining themselves as great explorers, "ready to receive a medal of honor for our courageous feat." The memory trails off, amid the reality of the courageous feat Amir still faces, without Hassan, who had always fought on Amir's behalf.

Outside the gates of the house, Amir notes that he feels "like a stranger." There are weeds, cracks in the pavement, peeling paint, broken windows, a sagging roof. Amir wants to go inside, to smell the familiar odors of the place and to listen to Hassan sing. Farid warns him that they must not linger, though, and that it is best to forget his past since nothing from it has survived. Amir responds, "I don't want to forget anymore," a sign that he is ready to face his past and make up for his former actions and behavior by helping Hassan's son.

Amir and Farid stay overnight in a badly damaged hotel where there is no hot water, no electricity, a broken window, and a dried bloodstain on the wall. As the two get ready to fall asleep, Farid tells a traditional Afghan joke and Amir thinks of how, amid all the changes to his homeland, Afghan humor has remained intact. The jokes go back and forth, and then Farid asks Amir his real reasons for coming back. Farid cannot understand why Amir would go out of his way for a Shi'a. Amir cuts off the conversation and stays awake wondering if Afghanistan might truly be a hopeless place.

At the stadium the next day, Amir, Farid, and the rest of the crowd watch a soccer game. At halftime, pickup trucks drive onto the field, where a man and a woman are each placed into their own chest-deep holes. A cleric recites from the Koran, and Amir remembers how Baba had railed against such figures. The cleric intones that God says that sinners must be punished. A man in a white robe and sunglasses, of the style popularized by John Lennon, enters the field. Farid says that he must be the man they need to talk to. The man stones the two in the holes.

Farid sets up a meeting with the man for three o'clock. In **chapter twenty-two**, Farid and Amir arrive for the appointment with the man from the stadium. Amir goes toward the house by himself. He is frisked by two armed men and left waiting in a room, wondering how he could have ended up in such a place, as he believes himself to be such a coward. While waiting, he eats a grape from the coffee table and relates that at the time he did not know it would be the last piece of solid food he would have for a while. This foreshadows the grim events to come.

The Talib man with the John Lennon glasses enters. He has his guards rip off Amir's fake beard. He asks Amir if he enjoyed "the show" earlier that day and then proceeds to brag to Amir about the massacre of the Hazara that had taken place not long after the Taliban secured Mazar, a city in Afghanistan that was one of the last to be taken.

The man asks if Amir has come from the United States. Amir answers that he has and that he has come for Sohrab. The Talib, though, returns to talk of the United States, calling it a whore. He explains that he could have Amir arrested for treason, and even shot, since he abandoned his country when it needed him.

The man has the guards bring Sohrab. Amir is surprised at how much the boy resembles Hassan. The Talib has made the boy wear makeup on his face and bells on his ankles. The man has him dance for them, and when the dance is done, the man wraps his arms around the boy and touches him inappropriately. The man then reveals his identity—he is Assef. He takes off the sunglasses, locking eyes with Amir.

Assef tells Amir how he came to join the Taliban. He and his father had been arrested, as were many others from the upper class, and abused in jail. Assef says he has since then been on a mission to clean Afghanistan, and when Amir tells him that in the West they call such activity ethnic cleansing, Assef actually finds the phrase appealing.

Assef says Amir can have Sohrab but that first they have some old business to address. He tells his guards to stay out of the room, no matter what, and that either he or Amir will walk out of the room alive. Assef takes out his brass knuckles.

The narrative then shifts. Amir describes a man in a surgical mask looking over him. We assume this is a glimpse into the near future, or potentially that Amir is imagining having to be operated on because he assumes he will be badly beaten.

Then the narrative focus returns to the room where the fight is imminent. Assef has said Sohrab should stay to watch, so the boy remains. Amir relates that he has never thrown a punch in his life, so he could not be much of an adversary for Assef. He says he remembers parts of the fight vividly. He remembers getting slammed with the brass knuckles, his jaw shattering, swallowing teeth, and ribs snapping. At one point he starts laughing because, for the first time since the day he had watched Assef abuse Hassan, he felt at peace and healed. He had finally gotten punished.

Sohrab, with tears rolling down his cheeks, calls for Assef to stop. He has his slingshot loaded and pointed directly at the Talib's face. The boy will not back down, and when Assef does not let go of Amir, Sohrab shoots the slingshot. Assef shrieks in pain and covers his eye. Sohrab takes Amir's hand to help him get away, and as they rush off Amir realizes that Assef has a brass ball, Sohrab's ammunition, stuck in his eye socket. Outside they still hear Assef's screams, as Farid runs toward Sohrab and Amir, picks up Amir, and guides him to the truck.

In **chapter twenty-three**, Amir is in the hospital, fading in and out of consciousness. He dreams of his father wrestling a bear but then realizes that it is not his father but he who is doing the wrestling. When Amir is more alert, he finds out that he has been in this hospital in Peshawar for two days and is lucky to be alive. The fight with Assef left him with a ruptured spleen; broken ribs; a punctured lung; a broken eye socket; and many cuts, including a lacerated upper lip, resembling the harelip that Hassan once had.

Farid and a reticent Sohrab come to the hospital the next day. Farid says Rahim has left his home but that the landlord gave Farid a letter and key to a safe deposit box that Rahim had left for Amir. Farid leaves Sohrab at the hospital for a while, but the boy has nothing to say when Amir tries to speak with him, and he looks down at his hands.

Later, by himself, Amir reads Rahim's note. Rahim writes that Hassan told him what had happened the day of the kite-flying contest shortly after it happened and that Amir should not be too hard on himself about it. He writes, "A man who has no conscience, no goodness, does not suffer."

Rahim writes that he is ashamed for having kept from Amir and Hassan the identity of Hassan's true father. He writes that Baba was "a tortured soul" because of his guilt about Hassan. Baba had wished he could love Hassan openly and took out his frustration on Amir. Explaining some of Baba's other actions, Rahim writes that he believes Baba wanted to redeem himself and so built the orphanage and performed other generous acts. Rahim writes that God will forgive them all, that Amir should try to forgive Baba and Rahim, but most of all that Amir must forgive himself.

When Farid comes to visit at the hospital again, he says it is probably not safe for Amir to be there for very long since allies of the Taliban will look for him. Farid advises that as soon as Amir can walk they should go to Islamabad. Amir asks him for another favor, and Farid brings Amir to tears by using the phrase Hassan first spoke to him: "For you a thousand times over." Amir asks Farid to look for the Caldwells, the people Rahim said would take care of Sohrab. Sohrab stays with Amir, and the two play cards. When Amir asks if they could be friends, the boy pulls away.

Amir takes his first steps that night, but they are slow and he is in great pain as a result. That night he dreams of Assef telling him that, while Amir and Hassan nursed from the same woman, it is actually Amir and Assef who are the same. Amir is not yet freed of the guilt he has long harbored from his youth.

Farid tells Amir that the U.S. consulate revealed that the Caldwells never existed. For now, Sohrab will go with Amir and Farid to Islamabad. On the way, Amir has many dreams and flashbacks, the last one of Rahim telling him there is "a way to be good again."

In **chapter twenty-four**, Farid, Amir, and Sohrab arrive in Islamabad. Amir thinks of it as the city that "Kabul could have become"; Sohrab is impressed by the famous Shah Faisal Mosque, which, Amir notes, is purported to be the largest mosque in the world. Farid takes Amir and Sohrab to a hotel and says he must return to his children. Outside the hotel Amir sees him off, giving him about two thousand dollars, which leaves Farid speechless.

Because Amir is still in great physical discomfort, he takes a pain pill and lies down. When he wakes up, Sohrab is gone. Amir drags himself to the front desk and asks the man there if he has seen the boy. Finally, Amir realizes Sohrab might have gone back to the mosque he had been intrigued with. The man at the desk agrees to give Amir a ride to the mosque because, he says, "I am a father like you." Apparently he sees how intensely worried Amir is, the way a parent would be.

Sohrab is, in fact, near the mosque, and he tells Amir he remembers going with his family to the Blue Mosque. He asks Amir if he misses his parents and asks if it is bad that he is starting to forget his own parents' faces. Amir assures him that it is not bad and gives the boy the photo of Hassan and Sohrab that Rahim had given him. Amir tells him he should keep it.

The boy says he has been thinking about mosques. He starts to cry and asks Amir if he will go to hell for using his slingshot against Assef. Amir reaches to comfort the boy but pulls back when the child flinches. Amir assures him he will not go to hell, then Sohrab asks if his father will be disappointed in him. Amir says Sohrab's father will be very proud, since Sohrab saved Amir's life. The boy cries for a long time and then says that even though he misses his parents, Rahim, and Sasa, he is glad they are not there to see how dirty he is. He says that the men who had been keeping him had done inappropriate things to him. Amir again assures him by telling him he is not tainted in any way. Amir tries to touch him again and the boy draws back once more, but when Amir tries a third time, more gently, the boy gives in and sobs in Amir's arms. Amir asks Sohrab if he would like to go to the United States to live with Amir and his wife, but the boy does not answer and continues to cry.

A week goes by, and Amir and Sohrab go for a picnic. Amir sees so many people enjoying the day and thinks of how Afghanistan is in ruins, how his own people are destroying it. Without thinking, Amir tells the boy that he and Hassan were brothers. Amir had wanted to tell the boy before, so he would not be hiding anything anymore. Amir explains, and when the boy asks if Baba was ashamed of Hassan, Amir answers that he thinks Baba was ashamed solely of himself.

Back at the hotel, Sohrab mentions San Francisco, and Amir tells him about it. Amir asks the boy if he has given any more thought of his offer to bring the child to the United States with him. Sohrab says he is afraid, since Amir could grow tired of him and his wife might not like him. Amir assures him that that would not happen. The boy says he does not want to go to another orphanage, and Amir promises that will never happen. The boy cries and nods his head, agreeing to go with Amir to live in the United States.

Amir calls his wife and tells her he is bringing a boy with him that he wants them to adopt. He tells Soraya the whole story of what had happened between him and Hassan. While he had thought of doing so many times in the fifteen years of their marriage and dreaded it, as he tells her then, he now feels a great relief. Soraya cries. She tells Amir that she knows the boy must come home with him.

Amir takes Sohrab to the American embassy in Islamabad. They meet with a man, Raymond Andrews, whom Amir dislikes from the start. After Andrews listens to Amir, he tells him he should give up on trying to adopt the boy, that it will be nearly impossible since by law it has to be proved that the boy is an orphan. When Amir goes to leave, he asks the man if he has any children and gets no response. Andrews asks if Amir has promised the boy he will take him and warns Amir that it is dangerous to make promises to children. Still, recognizing that Amir is truly determined, Andrews gives him the name of an experienced immigration lawyer, Omar Faisal. On the way out,

Amir tells the secretary how disappointed he is in Andrews, and she responds that the poor man has not been the same since his daughter committed suicide.

Amir calls Soraya and tells her Andrews's disheartening news, but she says her uncle, Sharif, who works for the Department of Immigration and Naturalization Services, is trying to help them.

Amir and Sohrab meet with Faisal, who is kind and gets Amir to tell the true story of how he has found Sohrab. Like Andrews, Faisal tells Amir he needs death certificates of the boy's parents. Also, he says that INS does not like to remove children from the countries in which they were originally living. Faisal advises that the best probable option is to send the boy to an orphanage and then file an orphan petition. When Amir explains this to Sohrab, Sohrab says Amir had promised him he would never have to go back to such a place. Sohrab is afraid he will be abused again and sobs, begging Amir to promise him he will not make him go to an orphanage. Andrews's comment seems to ring true, it is dangerous to promise things to children. Of course, Amir has had little experience with children and no experience as a father or father figure.

Amir is awakened by a phone call from his wife. She explains that Sharif can help them adopt Sohrab and that they can do so in a much easier way than what has already been described to Amir. Amir and Soraya are thrilled, and when Amir goes to tell Sohrab the good news, Amir pushes on the bathroom door then falls to his knees and screams.

In **chapter twenty-five** Amir watches Sohrab get wheeled into an operating room and rushes after him but is escorted out to wait. Distraught, Amir takes a sheet from a closet, finds out which way is west, gets down on the floor, and begins praying intensely through his tears. There must be a God, he tells himself, desperate and praying, making promise after promise to God. He writes that his hands are already stained with Hassan's blood and that they cannot be stained with the blood of his son as well.

Amir feels his chest tightening. He has been waiting for five hours without receiving news. The sight that prompted him to scream upon entering the bathroom is then revealed. He wishes it had been a dream when he saw Sohrab with his arm dangling over the side of the tub, the bloody water, the bloody razor, and Sohrab's half-closed eyes.

Amir awakens, and the doctor tells him that Sohrab needed several units of blood, had to be revived twice, and is alive only because he is young and strong. Amir weeps in relief.

Beside the unconscious boy, Amir falls asleep. He dreams that the doctor comes to him, and when the doctor takes off his surgical mask, he is not the doctor at all but Andrews from the embassy—the man whose own child had committed suicide.

Several days elapse, and Amir goes back to his hotel. He thinks of what the manager had said to him when Amir had first arrived and told him he did not know where Sohrab was: "The thing about you Afghanis is that . . . well, you people are a little reckless." Amir wonders if he really did go to sleep after he had told Sohrab it would be best for him to go temporarily to an orphanage.

When Sohrab finally opens his eyes in the hospital, he does not speak; his face is like stone, his eyes empty. When Amir reads aloud part of Sohrab's favorite book, the *Shahnamah*, the boy remains unresponsive, although Amir is glad he at least shakes his head when asked him if he wants to hear more. Amir asks him how he feels, and the boy responds that he is tired, tired of everything, and that he wants his old life back. Feeling helpless, Amir thinks how he lived in the same house that Sohrab later occupied and how that life is gone, including the people they loved. Amir tells him he wishes he could get his old life back for him. The boy says he wishes Amir had left him in the tub, and Amir tells him how crushing that is to hear.

Amir touches Sohrab's shoulder, and the boy flinches and pulls away, reminding Amir of how he had managed to comfort the boy with his touch in the days before Sohrab's suicide attempt. Amir tells Sohrab he can now bring him to the United States by a different method, and he begs the boy to forgive him for breaking his promise about the orphanage. Amir asks Sohrab again if he will come to the United States, but the boy only turns away and repeats how tired he is. Amir realizes everything is changed. He did not know at the time that it would take almost a year for Sohrab to speak again.

Amir takes the boy to the United States. The narrative references a memory of Amir's, of when he first realized Americans do not like to be told in advance what happens at the end of movies. He thinks that if someone asked him about the ending of the story of him, Hassan, and Sohrab, whether it turned out to be happy or not, that he would not know what to say, "despite the matter of last Sunday's tiny miracle." In short, the reader now knows that as the narrator writes his story, he is thinking back to a positive event that has just occurred.

Amir describes what it was like to arrive home "about seven months ago" in August 2001. Sohrab is stonefaced, and when Amir looks in on him that night he sees the photo he had given him of Hassan and Sohrab. Amir thinks about how Baba had probably thought of Hassan as his real son, and Amir realizes that such thoughts no longer brought pain. Forgiveness for his father has finally replaced it.

When Amir's in-laws come to dinner to meet Sohrab, the general asks what he is to tell the neighbors who are wondering why a Hazara boy is living with his daughter. Amir explains who Sohrab is, holding nothing back, and adds, "You will never again refer to him as 'Hazara boy' in my presence. He has a name and it's Sohrab."

Sohrab lives silently, never speaking. Meanwhile in the world at large, great changes have occurred after the attack on the World Trade Center and the U.S. bombing of Afghanistan. People were hopeful as Hamid Karzai was put in charge of their war-torn land. Amir and Soraya become involved in Afghan projects. They help raise money for a small hospital that had closed down near the Afghan–Pakistani border.

Amir then relates that four days ago, in March 2002, "a small, wondrous thing happened." He, Soraya, Sohrab, and his mother-in-law attend a gathering of Afghans at a park. It rains, and they huddle under a makeshift tent. Various men tell Amir how Baba had deeply affected them and that Amir was "lucky to have had such a great man for a father." The rain stops, and Soraya points to some kites in the sky. Amir buys a kite and brings it to Sohrab, telling him some stories about kites as Soraya tensely looks on. She had long ago stopped trying to speak with the boy, although Amir had never given up.

Amir tells the boy how his father would check the wind when he and Amir would fly kites, how Hassan was one of the best kite runners. Amir asks if Sohrab wants to help him fly the kite, but the boy does not respond. Amir gets the kite aloft and feels like a child again, realizing that Sohrab is next to him. He holds out the string, and the boy takes it. Amir writes, "I wished time would stand still."

Amir sees a green kite close by and tells Sohrab they need to go after it. Amir realizes Sohrab is alert and then wonders "when I had forgotten that, despite everything, he was still just a child." Amir watches as the spool of string rolls in Sohrab's hands, and just briefly Amir sees Hassan's hands and recalls parts of his own childhood. Amir tricks the other kite flyer and then moves in and cuts the kite down. The crowd cheers, whistles, applauds, and Amir sees a very small smile on one side of Sohrab's face. It leaves in an instant, but Amir focuses on the fact that it was there. He asks Sohrab if he should run after the falling kite for him, and when Amir thinks he sees the boy nod, Amir tells him, "For you, a thousand times over," and runs, thrilled at the smile, hopeful that it is a beginning. He runs with the other children, sporting an enormous grin.

Critical Views

Behind the title of first novelist Khaled Hosseini's "The Kite Runner" lurks a metaphor so apt and evocative that even the author never fully exploits its power. For the benefit of readers who didn't grow up in Afghanistan—as Hosseini and his alter ego Amir did—a kite runner is a sort of spotter in the ancient sport of kite fighting. In a kite fight, competitors coat their kite strings in glue and ground glass, the better to cut their rivals' moorings. While the fighter's kite is swooping and feinting in an effort to rule the skies, his kite-running partner is racing to own the streets, chasing down all their opponents' unmoored, sinking trophies.

It's a fresh, arresting, immediately visual image, and Hosseini uses it well enough as a symbol for Amir's privileged Afghan childhood in the 1970s, when he and his faithful servant, Hassan, had the run of Kabul's streets. Near the novel's end, when the adult Amir returns in secret to Taliban-controlled, sniper-infested Kabul in search of Hassan's lost son, the contrast with his cosseted, kite-flying youth could scarcely be more pronounced, or more effective.

But Hosseini could have deepened the symbolism even further if he hadn't ignored what, in essence, a kite fight really is: a proxy war. Here's Afghanistan, jerked around like a kite for most of its 20th century history by the British, the Soviets, the Taliban and us, played off against its neighbors by distant forces pulling all the strings, and Hosseini never once makes the connection. It's just too tempting a trick to leave on the table.

Of course, it's Hosseini's metaphor and he can do with it—or not do with it—as he pleases. Considering how traditionally and transparently he tells the rest of Amir's story, though, Hosseini wouldn't seem the type to go burying half-concealed ideas for readers to tease out. More likely, he instinctively hooked a great image but, alas, doesn't yet have the technique to bring it in for a landing. It's a small failing, symptomatic of this middlebrow but proficient, timely novel from an undeniably talented new San Francisco writer.

Hosseini's antihero Amir narrates the book from the Bernal Heights home he shares with his wife, Soraya. Like Hosseini, Amir's a writer, modestly celebrated for literary novels with such pretentious-sounding titles as "A Season of Ashes."

But Amir's childhood in Kabul still haunts him, specifically his mysterious inability to earn the love of his philanthropically generous but emotionally withholding father, and his guilt about failing to protect his angelic half-caste old kite runner, Hassan, from a savage assault. When Amir receives a deathbed summons from his father's business partner in Pakistan, he sees a chance to redeem himself from the secrets that have left him psychically stranded between Afghanistan and the United States.

Unfortunately, we know all this because Amir tells us, and not just once. Listen to him here, on the verge of his rescue mission over the Khyber Pass: "I was afraid the appeal of my life in America would draw me back, that I would wade back into that great, big river and let myself forget, let the things I had learned these last few days sink to the bottom. I was afraid that I'd let the waters carry me away from what I had to do. From Hassan. From the past that had come calling. And from this one last chance at redemption."

One might excuse all this melodramatic breathlessness as the reflexive self-examination of a character who, after all, writes novels with titles like "A Season of Ashes." But Amir's not the only one given to overly explicit musings.

His father's old partner goes in for it too, in a letter to Amir: "Sometimes, I think everything he [your father] did, feeding the poor on the streets, building the orphanage, giving money to friends in need, it was all his way of redeeming himself. And that, I believe, is what true redemption is, Amir jan, when guilt leads to good." A fine thing, redemption, but better implied than stated—let alone restated.

Hosseini shows a much more natural talent when he stops telegraphing his themes and lets images do the work for him. All the material about the Afghan expatriate community in

Fremont is fascinating, especially the scenes of Amir and his once-prosperous father making the rounds of weekend garage sales. They take all their underpriced finds to swap meets and resell them, thus augmenting the father's paltry income from his gas station job, so that Amir can study writing at Ohlone Community College. Maybe we've seen similar immigrant stories before—the defrocked Iranian colonel of Andre Dubus' "House of Sand and Fog" comes to mind—but Hosseini imparts a delicacy here that transcends any mere topical curiosity about Afghanistan.

Would "The Kite Runner" have been published if the United States hadn't briefly entertained an interest in all things Afghan? Maybe not, but sometimes decent books come out for the wrong reasons. Hosseini has taken the sorrowful history of his tragically manipulated birthplace and turned it into informative, sentimental but nevertheless touching popular fiction. For every misstep, as when he says that his father faced the loss of his former station "on his own terms" (whatever that tired, blurry phrase might mean), there's a grace note, as when a traumatized catamite is described as walking "like he was afraid to leave behind footprints."

In the annual literary kite fight for summer readers—with Afghanistan now well down any list of the nation's current preoccupations—Hosseini may wind up with his strings sliced out from under him. Just don't be surprised if his modest but sturdy storytelling skills, once cut loose from the crosswinds of a cynical seasonal marketplace, someday find their way to an updraft.

Edward Hower on Fierce Cruelty and Love

This powerful first novel, by an Afghan physician now living in California, tells a story of fierce cruelty and fierce yet redeeming love. Both transform the life of Amir, Khaled Hosseini's privileged young narrator, who comes of age during the last peaceful days of the monarchy, just before his country's revolution and its invasion by Russian forces.

But political events, even as dramatic as the ones that are presented in "The Kite Runner," are only a part of this story. A more personal plot, arising from Amir's close friendship with Hassan, the son of his father's servant, turns out to be the thread that ties the book together. The fragility of this relationship, symbolized by the kites the boys fly together, is tested as they watch their old way of life disappear.

Amir is served breakfast every morning by Hassan; then he is driven to school in the gleaming family Mustang while his friend stays home to clean the house. Yet Hassan bears Amir no resentment and is, in fact, a loyal companion to the lonely boy, whose mother is dead and whose father, a rich businessman, is often preoccupied. Hassan protects the sensitive Amir from sadistic neighborhood bullies; in turn, Amir fascinates Hassan by reading him heroic Afghan folk tales. Then, during a kite-flying tournament that should be the triumph of Amir's young life, Hassan is brutalized by some upper-class teenagers. Amir's failure to defend his friend will haunt him for the rest of his life.

Hosseini's depiction of pre-revolutionary Afghanistan is rich in warmth and humor but also tense with the friction between the nation's different ethnic groups. Amir's father, or Baba, personifies all that is reckless, courageous and arrogant in his dominant Pashtun tribe. He loves nothing better than watching the Afghan national pastime, buzkashi, in which galloping horsemen bloody one another as they compete to spear the carcass of a goat. Yet he is generous and tolerant enough to respect his son's artistic yearnings and to treat the lowly Hassan with great kindness, even arranging for an operation to mend the child's harelip.

As civil war begins to ravage the country, the teenage Amir and his father must flee for their lives. In California, Baba works at a gas station to put his son through school; on weekends he sells secondhand goods at swap meets. Here too Hosseini provides lively descriptions, showing former professors and doctors socializing as they haggle with their customers over black velvet portraits of Elvis.

Despite their poverty, these exiled Afghans manage to keep alive their ancient standards of honor and pride. And even as

52

Amir grows to manhood, settling comfortably into America and a happy marriage, his past shame continues to haunt him. He worries about Hassan and wonders what has happened to him back in Afghanistan.

The novel's canvas turns dark when Hosseini describes the suffering of his country under the tyranny of the Taliban, whom Amir encounters when he finally returns home, hoping to help Hassan and his family. The final third of the book is full of haunting images: a man, desperate to feed his children, trying to sell his artificial leg in the market; an adulterous couple stoned to death in a stadium during the halftime of a football match; a rouged young boy forced into prostitution, dancing the sort of steps once performed by an organ grinder's monkey.

When Amir meets his old nemesis, now a powerful Taliban official, the book descends into some plot twists better suited to a folk tale than a modern novel. But in the end we're won over by Amir's compassion and his determination to atone for his youthful cowardice.

In "The Kite Runner," Khaled Hosseini gives us a vivid and engaging story that reminds us how long his people have been struggling to triumph over the forces of violence—forces that continue to threaten them even today.

Loyal Miles on the Context for the Examination of Self

In his debut novel, *The Kite Runner*, Khaled Hosseini focuses on two deftly characterized relationships as a means of exploring the personal and cultural tensions inherent in being Afghan. As Amir, the novel's narrator, struggles to fulfill his father's exacting standards, Hosseini utilizes the father–son relationship to explore the qualities traditionally ascribed to Afghan men: physical prowess and courage, the ability to judge between right and wrong, and the willingness to risk their lives to save others from injustice. The tensions in this relationship also roughly mirror Afghanistan's struggle in the 1970s to maintain

53

a traditional sense of national identity in the face of government instability and eventual invasion by a foreign power. Broader elements of Afghan society, such as ethnic and class divisions, also make it impossible for Amir to consider Hassan, his closest childhood companion and family servant boy, a friend. The gradual unraveling of both relationships and Amir's eventual attempts to reconcile with his father and with Hassan provide a structure through which Hosseini compellingly examines Afghanistan's recent cultural and national history.

The Kite Runner primarily focuses on three significant periods in Amir's life: his Kabul childhood, his and his father's first years as immigrants in 1980s California, and Amir's 2001 return to Taliban-controlled Afghanistan. Each of these sections effectively foregrounds a different stage in Amir's sense of self-identity against the backdrop of a developing national history. In the first section of the novel, as Amir reflects on his childhood, he cannot separate his relationship with Hassan from his current feelings about Afghanistan, saying:

> I never thought of Hassan and me as friends either. Not in the usual sense, anyhow. Never mind that we taught each other to ride a bicycle with no hands, or to build a fully functional homemade camera out of a cardboard box. Never mind that we spent entire winters flying kites, running kites. Never mind that to me, the face of Afghanistan is that of a boy with a thin-boned frame, a shaved head, and low-set ears, a boy with a Chinese doll face perpetually lit by a harelipped smile.

Amir's conflicting feelings lead him to betray Hassan in a tragic confrontation with three older boys in the aftermath of Kabul's annual kite-fighting tournament in 1975. This betrayal, like many moments in *The Kite Runner*, resonates on two levels: On a personal level, the desire to win his father's approval drives Amir's actions; on a cultural level, the older boys, like Amir, are Pashtuns, while Hassan is Hazara, and their confrontation exhibits the deeply felt tensions between the majority and minority ethnic groups, respectively, in

Afghanistan. The guilt that follows this betrayal shapes much of the novel's narrative tone and connects Amir's troubled past with his sense of cultural identity as he equates Afghanistan to the disfigured, oppressed boy he himself betrayed.

In 1981, after a sharply rendered escape through the Khyber Pass inside a nearly airtight gasoline tanker, eighteen-year-old Amir and his father immigrate to America where Amir hopes for a new life unfettered by his troubled past. Ironically, this new life revolves around weekend trading in the Afghan section of the San Jose flea market, a setting in which traditional Afghan customs govern social interactions. After their initial meetings at the market, Amir decides to woo Soraya, the daughter of a former Afghan general. Here Amir must seek his father's guidance through the rituals associated with a traditional Afghan courtship and wedding. During this process, Amir begins to assimilate some of his father's customs and values, ultimately earning his father's approval:

> He watched me joking with [an elder Afghan], watched Soraya and me lacing our fingers together, watched me push back a loose curl of her hair. I could see his internal smile, as wide as the skies of Kabul on nights when the poplars shivered and the sound of crickets swelled in the gardens.

Through Amir's choice of imagery, Hosseini emphasizes that Amir's growing connection to his father includes his acknowledgment of their shared past in Afghanistan, an initial step in Amir's efforts to reconcile with the troubled personal past he associates with his native country and culture.

Following a summary of the early years of Amir's marriage, the narrative leaps ahead nearly two decades, a transition that brings the novel to Amir's attempt to redeem his past betrayal of Hassan. After learning of Hassan's execution by the Taliban, Amir determines to return to Kabul and rescue Hassan's orphaned son. This homecoming forces Amir to confront his youth in Kabul and the effects of continuous warring since his emigration from the city. Through the events that follow, Hosseini links Amir's self-acceptance with his present experience in Afghanistan by not allowing Amir to atone for his sins until completely surrounded and physically beaten by the literal ruins of the past that has for so long haunted him. Here too, Amir's cultural identity relies on the context of a traditional past juxtaposed against the realities of ethnic divisions and a war-fractured present.

Because of Amir's fast-paced narrative and the careful symmetry of event and detail, the novel's final chapters challenge the limits of realistic plotting as Hosseini emphasizes a symbolic intertwining of characters' individual experiences with the national experience of Afghanistan. Amir, the privileged former prince of an aristocratic Afghan family, must save the son of a companion betrayed both by Afghan culture and by Amir himself. In order to develop a more complete sense of self-identity, Hassan's son—paralleling Amir's experiences throughout the novel and Afghanistan's current efforts to rebuild—must reconcile with and transcend a vividly recent and tragic past. This paralleling of characters and culture concludes Hosseini's exploration of the fundamental tensions involved in forming an identity rooted in a multifaceted culture and an always-developing historical experience. It is this examination of self in the context of culture and history that makes Hosseini's *The Kite Runner* a compelling debut.

ARLEY LOEWEN ON REDEMPTION

What makes the novel so unique is Amir's ruthless self-revelation. Instead of the perpetual self-justification of greatness and the constant blaming of others for their evils, standard fare in Persian classics, here the main character draws away the veil of his soul. He sees himself and is shocked!

In their innocent childhood days, Hassan dreamt that the two of them were swimming in Qargha Lake north of Kabul. The crowds are screaming at them because a monster is after them. In the dream, there is no monster, only water. Now

Amir, in an hour of self-reflection, realizes, *"There was a monster in the lake. It had grabbed Hassan by the ankles, dragged him to the murky bottom. I was that monster."* (75)   ⟋ B, 2,9

Amir sees that life is much easier if one does not have to face reality and be reminded of one's cycle of lies, betrayals and secrets. He wishes Rahim Khan had "let me live on in my oblivion" (198). The author understands the bliss to live on in forgetfulness and to keep the past covered, but it is superficial and damning, merely a life of role-playing.

A further shocking hour of self-revelation comes in another dream where he watches an execution, *"He is tall, dressed in a herringbone vest and a black turban. He looked down at the blindfolded man . . . He takes a step back and raises the barrel. . . . The rifle roars with a deafening crack. I follow the barrel on its upward arc. I see the face behind the plume of smoke swirling in the muzzle. I am the man in the herringbone vest I woke up with a scream trapped in my throat"* (210). Amir wakes up to the horrifying truth that "the beast is inside all of us". . . .

MANY OTHER THEMES

The novel is laced with many other sub-themes that could become studies in themselves. The novel is not a satire of Afghan culture; however, the author challenges many cultural taboos. Amir learns the freedom of honesty, openness and being vulnerable, which may be shocking to many. He admits his own weaknesses, writes about his wife shameful past, yet he never indulges in the sensual.

The greatest shock comes when the general, Amir's father-in-law, wants to know about Sohrab's whereabouts. Amir is fed up with pretension and fabricating stories in order to cover up someone's so-called honor. And so, he simply states the facts, *"You see, General Sahib, my father slept with his servant's wife. She bore him a son named Hassan. Hassan is dead now. The boy sleeping on the couch is Hassan's son. He's my nephew. That's what you tell people when they ask"* (315).

The author pokes fun at his culture without being overly sarcastic. He alludes to the habit of exaggeration. *"lauf—that Afghan tendency to exaggerate—sadly, almost a national affliction; if someone bragged that his son was a doctor, chances were the kid had once passed a biology test in high school"* (11).

He hints at the cultural phenomenon of despondency and self-pity, especially in light of the last 25 years of disaster and suffering, *"we're a melancholic people, we Afghans, aren't we? Often we wallow too much in ghamkori and self-pity. We give in to loss, to suffering accepting it as a fact of life, even see it as necessary. Zindagi migzara, we say, life goes on"* (176).

In contrast to the daring openness in this novel, the author satirizes the pretension of his culture, which is best portrayed by the general who is now working in the flea market in Fremont. He is the prototype of superficial arrogance. He will not stoop down to do any kind of labor because it is below his dignity. His habits and behavior are crafted into an art form, in order to make a good impression on people. The general *"laughed like a man used to attending formal parties where he'd laugh on cue at the minor jokes of important people"* (121). The general's deportment and speech are manufactured, which, as Amir says, *"sounded to me the way his suit looked: often used and unnaturally shiny"* (123).

The author criticizes himself when he disapproves of the arrogant, westernized Afghans who never were really part of Afghanistan and are only returning now to make dollars. The taxi driver who takes Amir to Kabul accuses him of being a tourist in Afghanistan because he and his family lived aloof from the real Afghanistan.

The author exposes the double standard where young men are free to sleep around, but girls carry the burden of honor for the family. Soraya has experienced this first hand, *"Their sons go out to nightclubs looking for meat and get their girlfriends pregnant, they have kids out of wedlock and no one says a . . . thing. Oh, they're just men having fun! I make one mistake and suddenly everyone is talking about nang and namoos, and I have to have my face rubbed in it for the rest of my life."*

CONCLUSION

If the author has one clarion message it is this: You overcome evil by doing good. One could easily slip into the simplistic conclusion that atonement comes through performing a list of good works. In other words, one can cover up evil, or make up for it by good deeds. Indeed, without the presence of the sacrificing figure of grace, Hassan, it would make light of the cost of making up for evil.

The reader who is looking for political symbolism in the novel will be disappointed. In my view, this is not a political novel. Nor is it the regular dribble of someone struggling for identity, nor the typical, rather predictable story of heroes fighting outside evil forces who have destroyed the country. Yet, it would be unrealistic if the author had not placed his story in the context of the last 25 years of war and civil strife. A statement like "*my countrymen were destroying their own land*" (280) is true and fits the novel, but it is not belabored.

Having said it is not a political statement, we can, however, interpret the novel as a clear social statement. It is not only a confessional of one person, but it reads as a didactic call to society to become honestly aware of their past and see how they can atone for their sins. It is, indeed, a very moralistic and intentionally pedagogical novel. The reader is called to seek redemption from whatever his past may have been and experience grace, which can lead him to overcome his own evil by being spurred to true goodness.

Mir Hekmatullah Sadat on Husseini's Unveiling of Afghanistan

While the novel is an easy read, the themes require plenty of attention and willingness to tackle multidimensional problems. The book can be read as a three-part novel. In the first part, Hosseini engages in nostalgic childhood recreation of a lost Afghanistan during the last days of the monarchy of Zahir Shah and the regime that overthrew him. The second part explores emigration during the Soviet occupation of Afghanistan and the tragedies of a displaced and tired people living in cultural bubbles of the past; it describes the process of migration and character of the expatriate community. The last part explores the Taliban's Afghanistan. It deals with the horror humans can inflict on other humans and stresses the underlying tone of standing up to repression. . . .

Throughout the novel, the reader is exposed to many characters. Hosseini creates some heroic characters such as Amir's father, Baba, the bear wrestling, honest, and respected Pashtun who distrusts the mullahs (clerics); while Rahim Khan a progressive, social conscious friend of Baba dances in the streets celebrating the false hope for peace in the Taliban takeover of Kabul ending the ethnic warfare of the mujahidin guerrilla factions. However, the Taliban regime's draconian edicts on women, education, and even kite flying force Rahim Khan to flee for Pakistan.

In addition, the antagonist Amir overcomes his fear, pride, and his father generation's hypocrisy to right the wrong, while Hassan represents their lost innocence. Hosseini balances these characters with some demonic characters such as Asif, a bully who evolves into an unbelievably brutal Taliban official. In hindsight, Hosseini wished he had added more humanity to Asif because he is too terrible to be considered human at all. By the same token, Afghan history is not that simple but a complex jigsaw of interrelated equations.

Sometimes ethnic and linguistic ties outweigh every other variable, and then at other times regional ties prove to be stronger than ethnic ties. Among Afghans in the Western Diaspora, discussing the dilemmas of divisive norms has become a taboo. When such topics are addressed all meaning is lost in falsified statements and words. There is also an attempt by some to silence topic in order to prevent discussion of ideologies or groups who wittingly brought desolation. Hence, denying the fact that there was ever such a design in Afghanistan when in fact most societies underwent such obstacles.

In contrast, Hosseini's approach is not discreet as *The Kite Runner* slices through skin and flesh to expose the socio-political and economic skeleton, which has beleaguered a nation-state formation in Afghanistan. Those acquaint with Afghan history know group conflict has existed since Afghanistan's inauguration in 1747.

CONCLUSION

Regrettably, the dreaded devil's spiral between victim and victimizer resulted in various factions committing terrible atrocities under the name of ethnicity and religion in Afghanistan. Partly to be blamed are ancient tribal traditions like "badal" (blood vengeance), use of religion for personal gains, and ethnocentrism evident in Afghan history (as discussed earlier) which have prevented the establishment of a compassionate regime. Like Amir, some Afghans not involved stood by watching, either helplessly or indifferently, or fled Afghanistan.

Many have tried telling the story of Afghanistan but usually flinging a burqa (veil) over her true face. Hosseini has cast that burqa off and describes in detail every wrinkle and birthmark. A famous Afghan proverb says, "If you do not like the image in the mirror do not break the mirror but break your face."

It is up to Afghans to decide whether they wish to break their face and disintegrate Afghanistan or accept it as their own self-reflection given its many flaws. Indeed, the image reflected is one of loyalty and betrayal as much as it is about redemption and ignorance. Nonetheless, Afghans must know that no amount of superficial doctoring at the skin-level will resolve the deep-rooted issues beneath the surface. Hosseini wrote in an email:

> The romanticized Afghanistan that lives in the minds of our parents (and in my own childhood memory) probably never existed. That society had warts and pimples that no one talked about and that strangely, no one talks about to this day. But I am glad that this book is reaching so many people. I get e-mails from readers thanking me for finally putting a human face to the Afghans. I don't know if I've done that, but it is true that our people have been—in fiction at least—faceless and voiceless for far too long.

For many who were born or raised in exile, this face presents itself as an opportunity to live memories, the happy as well as the sad, considering the Afghan Diaspora's loss of touch with Afghanistan. This trend can only be described as time warped "bubble communities" who live for the nostalgia of their era of success in Afghanistan.

In showing the unveiled face of Afghanistan, Hosseini, indirectly, criticizes the pre-war era which some proudly claimed "an era where no one's nose was broken" as being nothing but a superficial façade. The deceptive lure of Afghanistan's peacetime bears the roots of conflict. Many keep themselves, consciously or unconsciously, oblivious to the cruel institutional, social, and political repression. Individuals who only exercised their rights to speak and write and had not committed any crimes spent years in the prison cells where they were subjected to all methods of torture. Imprisonments and killings of common people and innocent intellectuals were still order of the day. The transition from peace to war is never easy or one-sided, for this purpose the surface issues touched upon by Hosseini's contribution comes from an underrepresented side of a complex episode. Most notably since this novel would most likely never been allowed by the government to be printed during peacetime Afghanistan.

Afghans are notorious for falsifying preferences by publicly lying and privately being truthful about their persuasions based on sectarianism, religious and political bigotry. Like a medical doctor, Khaled Hosseini starts this sometimes excruciating healing process by opening the debate into the most pressing social diseases plaguing Afghans: ethnic-religious relations, the dichotomy of the privileged and unprivileged, the double standard for men and women, and the hypocrisy of those hiding their sins under the cloak of religious righteousness.

Hosseini's writing challenges those still living in the tribal mindset to gain courage and break away from their ethnic and clan affiliations, like Amir atone for sins, and join in the national reconciliation. Silencing the voices of the oppressed under the guise of a half-hearted "national unity" is the continuation of oppression manifested like the bone-crushing whips of the Vice-Virtue Police of the Taliban. Wounds of the whip, whether physical or social, do not heal if they are masked or unacknowledged. If we do not remember the past, we cannot forgive the past and work towards the future.

References

Adamec, Ludwig. (2003). *Historical Dictionary of Afghanistan.* Maryland: Rowman & Littlefield.

Ghobar, M.G.M. (1967). *Afghanistan dar Masir-e Tarikh*, Volume I. Kabul, Afghanistan.

Gregorian, Vartan. (1969). *The Emergence of Modern Afghanistan.* California: Stanford University Press.

Hosseini, Khaled. (2003). *The Kite Runner.* New York: Riverhead.

Noelle, Christine. (1997). *State and Tribe in Nineteenth-Century Afghanistan.* Britain: Curzon Press.

RONNY NOOR ON SOME OF THE NOVEL'S LIMITATIONS

This lucidly written and often touching novel gives a vivid picture of not only the Russian atrocities but also those of the Northern Alliance and the Taliban. It is rightly a "soaring debut," as the Boston Globe claims, but only if we consider it a novel of sin and redemption, a son trying to redeem his father's sin. As far as the Afghan conflict is concerned, we get a selective, simplistic, even simple-minded picture. Hosseini tells us, for example, that "Arabs, Chechens, Pakistanis" were behind the Taliban. He does not mention the CIA or Zbigniew Brzezinski, the national security advisor to President Carter, "whose stated aim," according to Pankaj Mishra in the spring 2002 issue of *Granta*, "was to 'sow shit in the Soviet backyard.'"

Hosseini also intimates that the current leader handpicked by foreign powers, Hamid Karzai—whose "caracul hat and green chapan became famous"—will put Afghanistan back in order. Unfortunately, that is all Karzai is famous for—his fashion, Hollywood style. His government does not control all of Afghanistan, which is torn between warlords as in the feudal days. Farmers are producing more opium than ever before for survival. And the occupying forces, according to human-rights groups, are routinely trampling on innocent Afghans. There is no Hollywood-style solution to such grave problems of a nation steeped in the Middle Ages, is there?

If *The Kite Runner*'s early adopters picked up the book to learn something about Afghanistan, what kept them reading (and recommending it) is the appealingly familiar story at the heart of the novel: a struggle of personal recovery and unconditional love, couched in redemptive language immediately legible to Americans. *The Kite Runner* tells the story Amir and Hassan, two childhood best friends in Kabul, divided by class and ethnicity. Amir is a wealthy Pashtun, and Hassan, his servant, is a *Hazara*. Hassan is a child of preternatural goodness and self-confidence, though he is illiterate and often picked on by roving Pashtun boys, in particular a "sociopath" named Assef. Amir, whose mother died in childbirth, is an outsider ill-at-ease with himself. He is debilitatingly hungry for the love of his father, Baba, a wealthy businessman who is puzzled that his son prefers reading to watching soccer. The studiously symmetrical plot revolves around an act of childhood cowardice and cruelty that Amir—the narrator—must make amends for years later, after he and Baba have emigrated to America. "There is a way to be good again," a friend counsels him. It's clearly such messages of redemption that prompted one Amazon reviewer to observe that *The Kite Runner* "remind[s] us that we are all human alike, fighting similar daily and lifelong battles, just in different circumstances."

The problem is that this last qualifying phrase, "just in different circumstances," underscores how uneasily the two different aspects of the book—the journalistic travel guide approach and the language of redemption—rub against each other. This is a novel simultaneously striving to deliver a large-scale informative portrait and to stage a small-scale redemptive drama, but its therapeutic allegory of recovery can only undermine its realist ambitions. People experience their lives against the backdrop of their culture, and while Hosseini wisely steers clear of merely exoticizing Afghanistan as a monolithically foreign place, he does so much work to make his novel emotionally accessible to the American reader that there is almost no room, in the end, for us to consider for long what might differentiate Afghans and Americans.

The tidy "I'm being healed" trajectory that animates Amir's narrative is derived from a vocabulary of psychotherapeutic spiritual recovery that looks pretty threadbare when the predicament is the much messier one of a nation ravaged by political and religious war. This is hardly a book that whitewashes violence (several young boys are raped, and a woman is stoned to death), but the silver-screen melodrama of its central story line wishfully cuts against the fact-based horrors depicted within. Near the end of the book, Amir tries to make amends for his old act of betrayal by saving Hassan's orphaned son from a Talib warlord who has kidnapped him, and who is portrayed as a bloodthirsty would-be Hitler. The warlord turns out to be Assef—the childhood nemesis who had tormented Hassan. When Assef rhapsodizes about taking the "garbage" out of Afghanistan—a reference to the slaughter of Hazaras by the Taliban—Amir challenges him with a note so smugly struck it leaves a bad taste in the mouth, even though we agree with his disgust: "In the west, they have an expression for that," I said. "They call it ethnic cleansing." The Hollywood elements of his story conduce to a view of Afghanistan and its dilemmas that is in the end more riddled with facile moralizing than even the author may realize.

Because *The Kite Runner*'s didactic lessons are the precise sort we are hungry to hear (redemption is possible, Western values are exportable, and so forth), it is worth being alert to what's missing from the novel, which is much exploration of the subtleties of assumptions that do divide people. "I started the book wondering if there were going to be a lot of differences between my perspective as a liberal Christian and a Muslim perspective," one book-club reader told her local newspaper. "I found that there's a lot in common. Amir comes to a point when he is desperate, he reaches to God. To me, that's the way people within Christianity are." Study the 631 Amazon reviews and scores of newspaper features about *The Kite Runner*, and you'll find that most fail to mention that the narrator converts from a secular Muslim to a devoutly practicing one. Hosseini's story indulges this readerly impulse to downplay what is hard to grasp and play up what seems familiar. In the drama of the novel, Amir's conversion isn't a sign of his adherence to a particular set of theological beliefs, but of a generalized spirituality reflecting his moral development over the course of the novel. As the *Denver Post* reviewer was all too happy to reassure readers, "This isn't a 'foreign' book. Unlike Boris Pasternak's *Dr. Zhivago*, Hosseini's narrative resonates with familiar rhythms and accessible ideas."

One shouldn't underrate the complexity of the task facing Hosseini, who understandably wanted to make the human predicament at the core of his novel seem universal, not remote. There's something to be said for *The Kite Runner*'s strategy. This is a book you would never accuse of succumbing to the Orientalist fallacy—the West's tendency, as Edward Said has argued, to see Islamic society as fundamentally other (and implicitly inferior) to Western culture, and the embodiment of *an* exotic "Oriental" mind. Members of the Afghan community in America have praised *The Kite Runner* for its verisimilitude. (One mention of the novel on an Afghan discussion forum quickly led to a lively debate about Afghanistan's best kite fighters.)

But surely there is a middle ground. In *Imaginary Homelands*, a collection of essays, Salman Rushdie argues that the expatriate writer's vision of his homeland is necessarily suspect and that all novels of exile are a type of "broken mirror," complicated by nostalgia and wishfulness. He goes on to suggest that the exiled writer's duty is to be self-conscious about the ways his story is a partial one. Such a provisional, highly fictionalized vision, Rushdie argues, is paradoxically more accurate than any account that earnestly purports to capture an objective or "informative" depiction of national character or culture. Hosseini could benefit from a little more of this line of thinking. At the time of writing, he hadn't been to Afghanistan in 26 years, but he told one newspaper, "I tried to make a statement larger than what was going on in the book. What happened after the Soviet war is that the world just kind of packed its bags and went home and watched as the Afghans were brutalized." *The Kite Runner* may offer an unsparing portrait of ravage and despair. But it purveys an allegory of redemption and healing that, despite the seemingly unmediated realism of the atrocities it describes, is far too neatly reflected in the novel's tidy mirror.

JUDI SLAYDEN HAYES ON VISIONS OF TIME

In the real world—even in most fiction—people don't live the same day over and over, but they do go through cycles trying to figure out what they're doing and why. Amir is a prime example.

All of his life Amir tries to get Baba's attention and to please him. Baba doesn't like Amir's interest in poetry, reading, and writing. He doesn't like his lack of aggression. When Baba builds the orphanage, Amir thinks those children are getting all of Baba's attention, so he tells Baba he has cancer. Baba doesn't even acknowledge him. He does get Baba's approval when he wins the kite-fighting contest, but because of his cowardice when Hassan is raped, his victory is never satisfying. In America Baba is pleased with Amir and affirms his educational progress. But now everything is tainted by Amir's big secret sin.

After the day of the kite-flying contest, Amir has another agenda. No longer is he focused on Baba alone. Now he must deal with his sin. His first response is more sin. First it's small, rude behavior, avoiding the living reminder of what he's done, or bullying Hassan. None of that works, so he weaves a web of sin to rid his life of Hassan forever. He succeeds in removing him physically, but the ghosts of the past are always present.

Over time the two problems combine. When Amir is called to Pakistan by Rahim Kahn and hears what he is being asked to do, Amir has a choice to make. He can let the old cowardice take over, proving once again in his own mind that Baba was right about him after all, or he can risk everything and get out of the spiral of guilt and fear.

I wished Rahim Khan hadn't called me. I wished he had let me live on in my oblivion. But he had called me. And what Rahim Khan revealed to me changed things. Made me see how my entire life, long before the winter of 1975, dating back to when that singing Hazara woman was still nursing me, had been a cycle of lies, betrayals, and secrets.

There is a way to be good again, he'd said.

A way to end the cycle. (*The Kite Runner*, 198)

Amir's story is just one example of the nature of circular time in *The Kite Runner*. In dozens of ways, life keeps repeating itself: the parallel lives of Ali and Baba, Hassan and Amir, and even Assef and Amir. Life keeps coming back on itself in lots of ways. The contrasts, comparisons, and cycles of life represented in *The Kite Runner* prompt a closer look at time and how we measure it. . . .

Such differences in looking at time are cultural. In *The Dance of Life*, Edward T. Hall wrote about the cultural rhythms of life.[2] Most people today live in structured environments. They create their own schedules rather than living by the natural rhythms of seasons and sun. Time relates to work hours, both our own and the businesses with whom we deal. We run our lives by schedules and deadlines. But even in our socially controlled way of measuring time, we find rhythms. And we mesh with the rhythms of our culture. Moving from one culture to another means an adjustment in the rhythms of time. For example, visiting Spain means dinner at ten o'clock at night and social activities until the morning hours, which then leads to the need for a siesta in the afternoon.

Hall distinguishes between monochronic time and polychronic time. Polychronic time focuses more on people and the completion of tasks than on schedules. Deadlines are less important than the journey, the process, the concerns of the individuals involved. Monochronic time is measured by moments. Time is measured—spent, wasted, gained, lost, made up, killed, running out, moving in slow motion. Human needs are less important than keeping the schedules. These two ways of relating to time may clash. Individuals may be drawn to polychronic time while living in a monochronic world. Entire cultures can be more monochronic or polychronic, and in a world of cross-cultural business and social relationships, such differences may be difficult to overcome.

The differences, however, go deeper. Some cultures see history as linear; others see it as cyclical. Does history repeat itself? Or is it always progressive? Are those who don't learn from history destined to repeat it? Or should businesses and governments focus only on the present and future? A cyclical perspective means that individuals and entire cultures periodically have another chance to deal with an issue and perhaps to do a better job than they did the first time. In linear time each event is new and presents a one-time chance to do something well or poorly.

The immediacy of the postmodern world creates a fascination with time. Moving from one year to the next may mean that to be accurate atomic clocks must readjust by fractions of a second. Individuals want what they want when they want it with little patience for waiting, planning for a future payoff, or delayed gratification. For example, people in linear, monochronic societies don't save well; they seldom take on projects that may take generations to complete, such as building a great cathedral; in fact, they have difficulty maintaining their infrastructure (such as levees) until the need is immediate; and they're never without a watch. Gandhi said there is more to life than increasing its speed.

Western societies tend to be more linear and monochronic; Eastern cultures tend to be more cyclical and polychronic. An Eastern orientation is evident in *The Kite Runner*. The characters go through cycles of opportunities to deal with the same issues in their lives. Amir has more than one opportunity to deal with pleasing his father, finding courage, dealing with his sin and guilt, and finding forgiveness and redemption. He finally gets it right but in doing so simply continues the cycle of life that now includes another generation.

Note

2. Edward T. Hall, *The Dance of Life: The Other Dimension of Time* (Garden City, N.Y.: Anchor Press/Doubleday, 1983).

FATEMEH KESHAVARZ ON "NEW ORIENTALISM"

The recent arrest in Iran of Haleh Esfandiari, director of the Middle East program at the Woodrow Wilson International Center for Scholars, has ignited a storm of protest around the Western world. To many Americans, it is but one more sign that Iran, in particular, and the Muslim Middle East, in general, are inhospitable to women and to freethinkers. For some years, America's popular reading list has bolstered that view, ignoring political complexities of the region in favor of a simple narrative.

Best sellers like Azar Nafisi's *Reading Lolita in Tehran: A Memoir in Books* (Random House, 2003), Khaled Hosseini's *The Kite Runner* (Riverhead Books, 2003), and Åsne Seierstad's *The Bookseller of Kabul* (Little, Brown, 2003) have enforced and embellished the one-sided picture of Middle Eastern culture. Call it the "New Orientalism."

In the 1970s, Edward W. Said's influential *Orientalism* (Pantheon Books, 1978) offered a decisive critique of entrenched Western assumptions that construed Europe as the norm, from which the "exotic" and "inscrutable" Orient deviates. Not infallible—but certainly profound and engaging—Said's views fired the imagination of such influential scholars as Homi Bhabha and Gayatri Chakravorty Spivak, now central to postcolonial and subaltern studies.

But a new version of earlier assumptions pervades our culture today. The old European Orientalist writers of the 18th through the 20th centuries treated Middle Eastern culture and people as having been great in the remote past, but devoid of complexity and agency in the present. The New Orientalists don't improve on that. Whether it is Nafisi's women reading Western literature in postrevolutionary Iran, a brave bookseller smuggling works into Seierstad's Taliban-run Kabul, or Amir's guilt at tolerating the rape and repression of his kite-runner friend in Hosseini's book, they all reduce the cavernous and complicated story of the region into "us" and "them" scenarios.

Make no mistake. We should protest the incarceration of any academic anywhere in the world who gets caught in the crossfire of political games. We all wish Esfandiari to be freed, but the danger is that we will color all of Iran, the country in which I was born and whose contemporary literature and culture are a delight to teach, with such actions. If we do, we will give less, not more, aid to the many intellectuals, scholars, and writers who, little known in the United States, make up a vibrant, multifaceted Iranian culture. Bottom line: Iran—like many other countries in the Middle East—is more than a country of victims and villains. It has much to offer the world.

What makes the old Orientalism and its newer version effective is that their sinister plots build on each other—and gradually seep into our daily accumulated fears. In Ghostly Matters: Haunting and the Sociological Imagination (University of Minnesota Press, 1997), the sociologist Avery F. Gordon explains that ghost stories are accounts of phantoms that disturb the reader with their overpowering presence. And yet their most distinct feature is that they are absent from view. Ghosts haunt us by not being there. And the New Orientalist literature has been producing ghosts in abundance. Muslim ghosts are large in number and perfectly wicked, suitable qualities for generating fear. They are old, so their past supplies material for nightmarish rereadings of history.

The memoirs, travel accounts, novels, and journalistic writings whose popular domain is haunted by Muslim ghosts vary in quality. Thematically, they stay focused on the public phobia: blind faith and cruelty, political underdevelopment, and women's social and sexual repression. They provide a mix of fear and intrigue—the basis for a blank check for the use of force in the region and Western self-affirmation. Perhaps not all the authors intend to sound the trumpet of war. But the divided, black-and-white world they hold before the reader leaves little room for anything other than surrender to the inevitability of conflict between the West and the Middle East.

An example is Nafisi, a visiting fellow at the Johns Hopkins University's Paul H. Nitze School of Advanced International

Studies, in Washington, whose memoir *Reading Lolita in Tehran* I use to analyze the New Orientalist approach in my book Jasmine and Stars: Reading More Than Lolita in Tehran (University of North Carolina Press, 2007). In the memoir, the professor of literature who is the book's narrator brings other women into her home to read Western classics. Outside the reading group, the author is angered by the preference that a male Muslim student exhibits for the protagonist in Maksim Gorky's Mother over Jane Austen's female characters. She says to Mr. Nahvi, the archvillain: "I am not comparing you to Elizabeth Bennet. There is nothing of her in you, to be sure— you are as different as man and mouse." The "good" professor, who appreciates Austen and Western characters, and the "bad" Iranian of today, who dislikes them, appear to be locked in eternal fight. What about the vast range of other Iranians who fall somewhere in between?

Reading Lolita in Tehran banishes what it cannot deal with. For example, it celebrates the power of literature for the women who gather to read the forbidden texts (although it would not have to have been as secretly as the book suggests) as evidence of women's resilience in the face of a revived patriarchy in post-1979 Iran. The least the book could do would be to mention a few contemporary Iranian women writers. It makes no such reference. The reader will not know that at the time this memoir was written, such prominent Iranian women writers as Shahmush Parsipur, Simin Danishvar, Moniru Ravanipur, and Simin Behbahani, to mention only a few, captured the imagination of readers and made it to the best-seller list in Iran. In *Reading Lolita in Tehran*'s narration of postrevolutionary Iran, such complex and towering Iranian women do not exist. . . .

Don't hold your breath, either, for the "scholarly" versions of the New Orientalist discourse. They replicate the disturbing features of their popular counterparts. Bernard Lewis's recent work What Went Wrong?: Western Impact and Middle Eastern Response (Oxford University Press, 2002) lumps together the entire Muslim Middle East as "a culture" in turmoil in order to contrast it with Christian Europe as the epitome of progress. Generally speaking, Lewis, a well-known scholar of Near Eastern studies, is hostile to his subject: the modern Middle Eastern Muslim. Omid Safi, an associate professor of religious studies at the University of North Carolina at Chapel Hill, counts, in an essay in the fifth volume of Voices of Islam (Praeger Publishers, 2007), 14 demeaning qualifiers, such as "poor," "weak," "ignorant," "humiliating," "corrupt," "impoverished," "weary," and "shabby," on one page. The menacing tone of Lewis's discourse, perpetuated in his punitive narrating voice, scolds Muslim subjects at every turn for their "fall" from glory. At the same time, while their supposed rage, ignorance, and incompetence are made hypervisible, a kind of background noise setting the ghostly ambience, they rarely speak for themselves. The absence of Muslim voices and commentators comes across as a natural function of their lack of dynamism and agency. . . .

Lewis closes with prescribing for the ghost a dose of the liberty enjoyed by those "schooled in the theory and practice of Western freedom." The list of recommended freedoms is long, but it does not include the one on the minds of Middle Easterners these days: freedom from military intrusion.

SHAFIQ SHAMEL ON THE NOVEL'S SOLUTION

In the following, I will mainly focus on Amir's character as its idealistic presentation forgoes exactly the central conflict to which *The Kite Runner* seems to present an imaginary solution. Given the political, social, and cultural history of what is now referred to as Afghanistan, the novel, in idealizing the figure of Amir, takes its point of departure exactly at a point that, from a historically reflexive perspective, it would have needed to arrive at. Needless to say that it will take enormous efforts in social-intellectual engineering, rather than mere recognition of blood relationship among various groups of people, in order to achieve both peaceful and respectful co-existence as well as social cohesion among different ethnic groups in today's Afghanistan.

The conflict-laden dynamics of Afghan society from within are mainly the result of the complex relation between the following paradigms of existence: ethnicity, religion, and language. Cultural identity and nationalism in the modern European sense are a function of the interplay among ethnic, religious, and linguistic affiliations. While it is almost impossible to determine with certainty which of these forces has the highest potential for triggering or fostering prejudice and discrimination among different groups of people, Hosseini's novel treats ethnic and religious affiliations as the source of injustice and socio-psychological imbalance in the Afghan society. The resolution that *The Kite Runner* offers for the present ethnic and religious conflicts in today's Afghanistan revolves around the recognition as equal of an oppressed Shi'a Hazara by a member of the ruling Sun'a Pashtoon. Linguistic and class issues as the source of conflict are almost entirely eliminated from the mix. This desirable outcome is justified in the novel at the level of blood relationship: Amir, a Pashtoon (the Pashtoons have been in the possession of the political power in Afghanistan for nearly two and half centuries by now), transcends existing ethnic and religious taboos only when he learns that Hassan, officially known as the son of their Hazara servants Ali and his wife, is his half-brother.

The recognition of kinship as a force to bring about tolerance, as exemplified in Amir's case, resonates with the way Lessing has framed religious tolerance in the *Nathan the Wise*. Yet, such a schematization is inevitably reductive against the background of the complexity of the recent history of Afghanistan. An imaginary resolution to the conflicts between the Pashtoons and the Hazaras, based on blood relation, cannot be the end of all the troubles that Afghan society has been going through for more than a century and half now. Such a tendency, following the ideals of the European Enlightenment, is certainly welcome. Given the atrocities committed by the almost exclusively Pashtoon Taliban, such as the ethnic cleansing of the Persian speaking Shi'a Hazaras, Amir in *The Kite Runner* is one of the most humane fictional characters to have entered the Afghan and Afghan-American literary imagination to date. However, the more difficult question facing reality, as well as its fictional representation, is how to transcend ethnic, religious, and linguistic differences in Afghan society on grounds other than blood relationship and other than a single person's act of benevolence. In other words, what could serve as a common denominator among various ethnic groups, the Shi'a and the Sun'a, the Persian and Pashtoo speakers, to be constitutive of the kind of cultural and political identity that could bring about not only peaceful coexistence but also social cohesion in Afghanistan? An awareness of blood relation among various peoples in Afghanistan is not a recent phenomenon. If not the majority, at least a considerable portion of the population has always known about it. The multi-ethnic texture of the Afghan population is not only a consequence of Afghanistan being at the crossroads of so many conquerors throughout the last fifteen centuries, including the Arabs, the Turks, and the Moghuls; kings and rulers in Afghanistan have fostered the custom to engage in (forced or voluntary) marital relations with various ethnic groups throughout the land in order to win their loyalty. So there is much historical and social resonance in what Hassan says to Amir within the framework of a childhood friendship: "For you, a thousand times over." History, however, has shown again and again that even fathers kill their sons or vice versa, and that brothers quite often get at each other's throats.

The idea that a Pashtoon would recognize a Hazara, within the narrative framework of "the lost son," as his equal nonetheless gives the conflict a humanistic outcome. As we know, fiction is certainly not a call for action. But we also know that in many cultures the epic has always been constitutive of the ways its audiences look at the world and choose one or the other path for their actions. For better or worse, imaginary writing and fiction does have the force to shape patterns of mind as well as of action. Hosseini's allusion to the *Shahnamah* is not literary in nature; the *Shahnamah* is presented in the novel as the most read and appreciated book by the protagonist, Amir. Ferdowsee's vision of the pre-Islamic Persian speaking lands in a mythological figuration has left its impression not only on Hassan's worldview, as he gives his son the name (Sohrab) of one of the heroes of the *Shahnamah*, but, what is more, Amir has been also deeply affected by the poem. Amir and Hassan are bound to each other through their shared experience of reading the *Shahnamah*. This bond between the two offers a different model of resolving the ethnic, religious, and linguistic conflicts in Afghanistan, one that goes beyond the recognition of a mere blood relationship.

Works by Khaled Hosseini

The Kite Runner, 2003.

A Thousand Splendid Suns, 2007.

Annotated Bibliography

Ansary, Tamim. *West of Kabul, East of New York: An Afghan American Story.* New York: Farrar, Straus and Giroux, 2002.

This work offers another personal perspective on being an Afghan American. Like Hosseini, Ansary spent much of his life in the United States (moving there when he was 16), where he thought often about Afghanistan, Islam, and fundamentalism. An e-mail he wrote on September 12, 2001, the day after the destruction of the World Trade Center, is estimated to have reached millions of readers within a week. It gained him enormous attention from the media and made him realize he could humanize Afghans for Americans.

Armstrong, Karen. *Islam, A Short History.* New York: Modern Library, 2000.

Covering 1,500 years of Islamic history, Armstrong, a scholar who has written several books about religion, provides information on Islam, especially relevant at a time when some people remain unclear about the tenets of this faith, due in part to excessive attention being paid to its radical fundamentalist aspects. The work ties the religion's growth to events in history and covers the impact of the faith through present times.

Azad, Farhad. "Dialogue with Khaled Hosseini." Lemar–Aftaab afghanmagazine.com 3, no. 4 (June 2004). Retrieved February 12, 2008 from http://afghanmagazine.com/2004_06/profile/khosseini.shtml

Hosseini explains in this interview how he wanted *The Kite Runner* to give a human face to Afghans. He reveals that although the book has gotten mostly positive reviews, some people have been disturbed by its frank portrayal of racism and ethnic prejudices (that existed even during the "Golden Era of sorts" of the 1960s and 1970s). Hosseini says that such prejudices have haunted the country for many years but need to be addressed so the nation can move ahead.

Changnon, Greg. "Books: The Reading Room: A Guide for Book Clubs: Political Upheaval, Class Tatter Boys' Friendship." *The Atlanta Journal-Constitution* Arts section (August 22, 2004): 5L, Sunday home edition.

Changnon calls *The Kite Runner* "epic in scope and intimate in emotions." He writes that it draws the reader into a ravaged Afghanistan and the lives of its inhabitants who have witnessed so much violence. As he covers various events in the book, Changnon brings up questions and topics that a book group could cover, encouraging readers to examine the novel's various images and descriptions more closely.

Coll, Steve. *Ghost Wars: The Secret History of the CIA, Afghanistan, and Bin Laden, from the Soviet Invasion to September 10, 2001.* New York: Penguin, 2004.

The text explains how, in the years before the September 11 attacks, the CIA's involvement with Afghanistan impacted the Taliban and Al Qaeda. The book looks back in great detail to events during the Carter, Reagan, and Clinton administrations. Coll, managing editor of the *Washington Post*, covered Afghanistan from 1989 to 1992 and gained access to an array of material, some of it previously classified.

Constable, Pamela. "Pilgrimages." *The Washington Post* Book World section (July 6, 2003): T3, edition F.

In this review, Constable comments on *The Kite Runner* as well as two titles written by Arab-American women, all of which, she argues, give readers a better understanding of Muslim Americans, their lives in the United States, and what they fled from in their native lands. She admires Hosseini's work, believing what makes it powerful is its "hard, spare prose." Afghan culture and history, she writes, are handled ably for an American audience in *The Kite Runner*, and although some incidents are "raw and excruciating to read . . . the book in its entirety is lovingly written."

Emadi, Hafizullah. *Culture and Customs of Afghanistan.* Westport, Conn.: Greenwood Press, 2005.

A nonfiction work, this text provides a brief history of Afghanistan from as early as 1000 B.C.E. and addresses many other aspects of life in the country, exploring the religious ideas of its people, their customs, and their perspectives on family and women. Discussion also centers on literature and the arts in Afghanistan and themes and subjects that have recurred through time.

Ferdowsi, Abolqasem. *Shahnameh: The Persian Book of Kings.* Dick Davis, trans. New York: Viking, 2006.

In *The Kite Runner*, the *Shahnameh* is the favorite book of some of the main characters. Written as a poem more than a thousand years ago, the text is the great epic of Persia, covering the beginning of the universe through the seventh century. It also includes myth and legend, weaving a tale of heroes, kings, love, morality, and more.

Hosseini, Khaled. "The Long Road Home." *Guardian* (December 15, 2007). Retrieved February 12, 2008, from http://books.guardian.co.uk/review/story/0, 2227662,00.html

In this piece, Hosseini describes his visit to Afghanistan, having not been there since 1976. He had heard plenty of stories about what it was like but wanted to see for himself. He was struck by the hardship and poverty yet also heartened by the people's insistence on retaining dignity and hope.

Mendoza, Louis, and S. Shankar, eds. *Crossing into America: The New Literature of Immigration.* New York: New Press, distributed by W. W. Norton, 2003.

This book is an anthology of writings by immigrants and about immigration, using as a starting point 1968 (when legislative reforms went into effect in the United States and brought about a great influx of immigrants). The writing takes a variety of forms—essays, poetry, excerpts from fiction. Additionally, it includes a historical account of immigration in the United States, various cartoons and opinion pieces from newspapers, and part of a discussion held at the University of Texas at San Antonio.

Mills, Margaret A. *Rhetorics and Politics in Afghan Traditional Storytelling*. Philadelphia: University of Pennsylvania Press, 1991.

As Husseini notes in *The Kite Runner*, television was not a part of Afghanistan for some time; this and other factors kept alive a storytelling tradition, analyzed in this work. The author recognizes that the storytellers she meets with come from varied backgrounds, and she considers such differences while examining the tellers' choice of stories and aspects such as their themes, word choice, and character portrayals.

Milvy, Erika. "'The Kite Runner' Controversy." Salon.com (December 9, 2007). Retrieved February 12, 2008, from http://www.salon.com/ent/movies/feature/2007/12/09/hosseini/print.html

In this interview, Hosseini answers questions about the effect the attacks on the World Trade Center had on his book. Also, he describes events and people from his own life that he drew on to write the novel. Interviewed just prior to the release of the movie version of his book, Hosseini also discusses the controversy surrounding the film, which led its producers to take the young Afghan actors and their guardians out of Afghanistan.

Mousavi, Sayed Askar. *The Hazaras of Afghanistan: An Historical, Cultural, Economic and Political Study*. New York: St. Martin's Press, 1997.

Hosseini's *The Kite Runner* gives a clear vision of the intense prejudices against the Hazara in Afghanistan. In Mousavi's text, readers are introduced to these people and learn about their culture and beliefs, as well as their lives in different countries. Also described are various uprisings of the people and the results.

Orfalea, Gregory. *The Arab Americans: A History*. Northampton, Mass.: Olive Branch Press, 2006.

This text provides a historical perspective as well as a personal one on Arab Americans. The author amassed more than 150 interviews and discusses the waves of Afghan immigrants that arrived in the United States from 1878 to nearly present times. An entire chapter discusses how September 11 brought Afghanistan to the forefront for Americans. In that same chapter, Arab-American literature is discussed as well.

Pazira, Nelofer. *A Bed of Red Flowers: In Search of My Afghanistan*. New York: Free Press, 2005.

This memoir is by a female Afghan who stayed in her country until her family's escape in 1989. She remembers the beauty and ease of the 1970s in Afghanistan and the beginning of destruction when the Soviets invaded. Her father is jailed for refusing to join the communists, and Nelofer becomes part of the resistance. Her family eventually moves to Canada, but in 2002 Nelofer returns to Afghanistan to find out what has happened to an old childhood friend.

Roberts, Jeffery J. *The Origins of Conflict in Afghanistan*. Westport, Conn., and London: Praeger, 2003.

This text starts with Britain's policy on Afghanistan at the beginning of the 1800s. The work discusses leaders in Afghanistan but also how the nation was affected by events such as the partitioning of India and the U.S. alliance with Pakistan during the Eisenhower administration.

Sultan, Masuda. *My War at Home*. New York: Washington Square Press, 2006.

This memoir is written by an Afghan-American woman. Like Hosseini, she has been struck by returning to Afghanistan. Unlike Hosseini's character of Amir, though, who was taught to not follow religious teachings, Sultan grew up as a Muslim. Even though she lived in New York since age five, her family insisted on upholding certain traditions such as arranged marriage. The book tells of her rebellion against such practices and also of her quest to find herself.

Contributors

Harold Bloom is Sterling Professor of the Humanities at Yale University. He is the author of 30 books, including *Shelley's Mythmaking*, *The Visionary Company*, *Blake's Apocalypse*, *Yeats*, *A Map of Misreading*, *Kabbalah and Criticism*, *Agon: Toward a Theory of Revisionism*, *The American Religion*, *The Western Canon*, and *Omens of Millennium: The Gnosis of Angels, Dreams, and Resurrection*. *The Anxiety of Influence* sets forth Professor Bloom's provocative theory of the literary relationships between the great writers and their predecessors. His most recent books include *Shakespeare: The Invention of the Human*, a 1998 National Book Award finalist, *How to Read and Why*, *Genius: A Mosaic of One Hundred Exemplary Creative Minds*, *Hamlet: Poem Unlimited*, *Where Shall Wisdom Be Found?*, and *Jesus and Yahweh: The Names Divine*. In 1999, Professor Bloom received the prestigious American Academy of Arts and Letters Gold Medal for Criticism. He has also received the International Prize of Catalonia, the Alfonso Reyes Prize of Mexico, and the Hans Christian Andersen Bicentennial Prize of Denmark.

David Kipen is the director of literature at the National Endowment for the Arts. He is the author of *The Schreiber Theory: A Radical Rewrite of American Film History*. He is a former book critic for the *San Francisco Chronicle* and a former book critic and essayist for National Public Radio's *Day to Day*.

Edward Hower teaches writing at Ithaca College and was a Fulbright lecturer in India. He has written several works of fiction, including *The Storms of May* and *The New Life Hotel*.

Loyal Miles graduated from the University of Kansas and attended the creative writing program at Indiana University. His work has appeared in the *Cottonwood Review*.

Arley Loewen has been the Persian literature and culture specialist at the Central Asian Development Agency. He is the translator of *A Man Keeps His Word: Life and Culture in Kabul, Afghanistan* and has written for the *Journal of Afghanistan Studies*.

Mir Hekmatullah Sadat has taught at Pitzer College and has been a lecturer at the Naval Postgraduate School, where he taught Afghan history and culture, as well as issues such as cultural sensitivity, respect for Islam, treatment of civilians, and application of human rights to non-Americans.

Ronny Noor has written for *South Central Review*, *Journal of Pragmatics*, and *World Literature Today*. He has written many book reviews, commenting on, for example, *Electric Rhetoric* and *Virtual Lotus: Modern Fiction of Southeast Asia*.

Meghan O'Rourke is *Slate*'s literary editor and the author of *Halflife*, a collection of poetry. Her writing has appeared in *The New Yorker*, *Poetry*, the *New York Review of Books*, and elsewhere.

Judi Slayden Hayes is an editor and writer who has written for, contributed to, and edited books and magazines for publishers and organizations.

Fatemeh Keshavarz is professor of Persian and comparative literature and chair of the department of Asian and Near Eastern languages and literatures at Washington University in St. Louis. She is a translator, poet, and author of *Jasmine and Stars: Reading More Than* Lolita *in Tehran*.

Shafiq Shamel is a lecturer in the department of German studies and in the department of comparative literature at Stanford University. He is the author of *Goethe and Hafiz*.

Acknowledgments

David Kipen, "Pulled by the Past: An Immigrant Returns to Kabul in Bay Area Author's First Novel." From the *San Francisco Chronicle*, June 8, 2003, M-1. Copyright 2003 by the *San Francisco Chronicle*. Reproduced with permission of the *San Francisco Chronicle* in the format other book via Copyright Clearance Center.

Edward Hower, "The Servant ('The Kite Runner')." From *The New York Times*, book review, 108, August 3, 2003, p. 4. © 2003 by *The New York Times*. All rights reserved. Used by permission and protected by the Copyright Laws of the United States. The printing, copying, redistribution, or retransmission of the Material without express written permission is prohibited.

Loyal Miles, "The Kite Runner." From *Indiana Review* 26, no. 1 (Summer 2004): 207–209. © 1996–2008 by ProQuest LLC. Reprinted by permission.

Arley Loewen, "Not Worthy of His Sacrifice: An Overview of *The Kite Runner*." From Lemar-Aftaab afghanmagazine.com (June 2004). © Aftaabz Publications.

Mir Hekmatullah Sadat, "Afghan History: Kite Flying, Kite Running and Kite Banning." From Lemar-Aftaab afghanmagazine.com (June 2004). © Aftaabz Publications.

Ronny Noor, "Khaled Hosseini: The Kite Runner." From *World Literature Today* 78, nos. 3–4 (September–December 2004): 148. Copyright © 2004 by *World Literature Today*. Reprinted by permission. Visit the *WLT* Web site at wlt.ou.edu

Meghan O'Rourke, "*The Kite Runner*, Do I Really Have to Read It?" From *Slate*, July 25, 2005. © 2008 by Slate.com and Washingtonpost.com, Newsweek Interactive. All rights reserved.

Judi Slayden Hayes, "Living Life 'A Thousand Times Over.'" From *In Search of* The Kite Runner. Copyright 2007 by Christian Board of Publication. Reproduced with permission of Christian Board of Publication in the format other book via Copyright Clearance Center.

Fatemeh Keshavarz, "Banishing the Ghosts of Iran." From *Chronicle of Higher Education* 53, no. 45 (July 13, 2007). © 2007 by *Chronicle of Higher Education*. Reprinted by permission.

Shafiq Shamel, "Epic Poetry and *The Kite Runner:* Paradigms of Cultural Identity in Fiction and Afghan Society." From *Telos* 138 (Spring 2007): 182–184. © 2007 by *Telos.*

Every effort has been made to contact the owners of copyrighted material and secure copyright permission. Articles appearing in this volume generally appear much as they did in their original publication with few or no editorial changes. In some cases, foreign language text has been removed from the original essay. Those interested in locating the original source will find the information cited above.

Index